Prestwick House
LITERARY TOUCHSTONE CLASSICS™
P.O. Box 658 Clayton, Delaware 19938 • www.prestwickhouse.com

Senior Editor: Paul Moliken

Editors: Douglas Grudzina, Sondra Y. Abel, and Elizabeth Osborne

Cover Photography: Larry Knox

Layout & Production: Larry Knox

Prestwick House
LITERARY TOUCHSTONE CLASSICS™

P.O. Box 658 • Clayton, Delaware 19938
Tel: 1.800.932.4593
Fax: 1.888.718.9333
Web: www.prestwickhouse.com

Self-Reliance
Friendship
All references come from *Essays and Addresses by Ralph Waldo Emerson*, copyright 1906 by Scott, Foresman and Company.

Civil Disobedience
All references come from an undated republication of *Civil Disobedience*, published by the U.S. government.

Walden
All references come from *Walden or Life in the Woods*, copyright 1910 by Houghton Mifflin Company.

ISBN 978-1-60389-016-8

TRANSCENDENTALISM:

ESSENTIAL ESSAYS OF EMERSON & THOREAU

Including *Self-Reliance & Civil Disobedience*

CONTENTS

Notes

What is a literary classic and why are these classic works important to the world?

A literary classic is a work of the highest excellence that has something important to say about life and/or the human condition and says it with great artistry. A classic, through its enduring presence, has withstood the test of time and is not bound by time, place, or customs. It speaks to us today as forcefully as it spoke to people one hundred or more years ago, and as forcefully as it will speak to people of future generations. For this reason, a classic is said to have universality.

Reading Pointers

Reading Pointers for Sharper Insights

In order to understand the ideas that are expressed in the essays of Emerson and Thoreau, it is important to understand some fundamental concepts of Transcendentalism. When it began in New England in 1836, the Transcendentalist Movement helped create new ideas, literature, religion, culture, and philosophy. The Transcendentalists expressed ideas that were rebellious—the writers were protesting society's belief in intellectualism, the authority of classic works, and the supremacy of religious doctrine. While most members of nineteenth-century society were striving to conform to its culture, traditions, and laws, Transcendentalists believed that each person should rely on his or her own intuition and spiritual essence; in fact, this trust in the self was the only way to reach an ideal spiritual state.

As you read the essays in this book, notice how the authors deal with each of the following:

- **Nature**—To the Transcendentalist, Nature is the outward sign of inward spirit, expressing the "radical correspondence of visible things and human thoughts," as Emerson writes in *Nature* (1836).
- **Religion and Spirituality**—Nature and spirituality are closely linked in Transcendentalism. Notice how the authors allude to elements of Buddhism, Hinduism, and Unitarianism in their writings. It should be noted that these religions focus more on spirituality than on doctrine and dogma.
- **Government**—Transcendentalists rebelled against popular notions of government and institutions because these entities sought to control the minds and lives of individuals. Thoreau, throughout his life, was against slavery (he was a strong supporter of the Underground Railroad); he also accepted imprisonment rather than paying a tax that supported the Mexican War, which he felt was unjust.
- **Education**—It is interesting to note that both Thoreau and Emerson attended Harvard, but later rebelled against its institutions and practices. Many Transcendentalist ideas and philosophies were aimed at changing the opinions of the intellectuals of that time.

- **Allusions**—Both Emerson and Thoreau allude to contemporary events, Greek and Latin mythology, Sanskrit scriptures, Chinese philosophy, earlier writers and philosophers, and biblical stories. A glossary has been provided at the end of each essay to identify many of these important references.

Also, notice how idealistic the authors are. Emerson himself acknowledges this fact and writes that pure Transcendentalism is impossible to attain in practice. However, these ideas are important because they have shaped thoughts and influenced many scholars, philosophers, and political leaders throughout the world.

Walden Pond, Concord, Massachusetts.

RALPH WALDO EMERSON

Ralph Waldo Emerson

Ralph Waldo Emerson, the founder of the Transcendentalist Movement, was a philosopher, activist, and author, as well as a guide and patron of other writers, especially his friend Henry David Thoreau. Emerson's Transcendentalism embraced some principles of Christianity, Eastern religions, and the English Romantics, but was not a subcategory of any of them; instead, it was a new, truly American philosophy, with the idea of self-reliance at its core.

Emerson was born in Boston. His father and grandfather were both Unitarian ministers, and the call to preach is clearly evident in Emerson's writing. However, he advocated a break with some of the formal teachings of the Unitarian Church. For instance, he caused an uproar while giving the graduation address at Harvard Divinity School when he disavowed the divinity of Jesus. Although Jesus was a good, insightful man who saw the truth clearly, said Emerson, Jesus was not God, and focusing on Jesus' divinity had done harm to the Church. Instead of blindly worshipping, each person should attempt to perceive the truth as clearly as Jesus had.

Emerson helped edit the magazine, *The Dial*, which published many Transcendentalist writings in the 1880s, and his first book of essays, *Nature*, (1836) was one of the most important publications of the Transcendentalists. In it, Emerson espouses the belief that human beings are connected to everything in the natural world by a common soul and states that all human beings have access to this soul through their own intuition; there is no need, he says, to get truth from books or higher authorities. He would elaborate upon this idea in *Self-Reliance,* his book of essays.

Although he claimed that travel is seldom worthwhile (because any knowledge can be gained at home), Emerson did travel to several continents, and he crossed America as a lecturer. While in England, he met several important poets of the Romantic Movement, including William Wordsworth and Samuel Taylor Coleridge. Their writing, like Emerson's, stressed the importance of individual intuition and the importance of finding solace in the natural world.

Emerson was married twice; his first wife, however, died of tuberculosis at the age of nineteen. With his second wife, Lydia (he called her Lidian), he had five children. The oldest, Waldo, died of scarlet fever at the age of five, and both parents suffered great emotional stress because of it.

Ralph Waldo Emerson died from pneumonia on April 27, 1882. The bells in Concord rang 79 times—one for each year of his life.

Self-Reliance

Ne te quaesiveris extra.[†]

Man is his own star; and the soul that can
Render an honest and a perfect man,
Commands all light, all influence, all fate;
Nothing to him falls early or too late.
Our acts our angels are, or good or ill,
Our fatal shadows that walk by us still.

Epilogue to Beaumont and Fletcher's Honest Man's Fortune.[†]

Cast the bantling on the rocks,
Suckle him with the she-wolf's teat,
Wintered with the hawk and fox.
Power and speed be hands and feet.

I READ THE OTHER day some verses written by an eminent painter which were original and not conventional. Always the soul hears an admonition in such lines, let the subject be what it may. The sentiment they instil is of more value than any thought they may contain. To believe your own thought, to believe that what is true for you in your private heart is true for all men,—that is genius. Speak your latent conviction, and it shall be the universal sense; for always the inmost becomes the outmost—and our first thought is rendered back to us by the trumpets of the Last Judgment.[†] Familiar as the

[†]Terms marked in the text with (†) can be looked up in the Glossary for additional information.

voice of the mind is to each, the highest merit we ascribe to Moses,† Plato,† and Milton† is that they set at naught books and traditions, and spoke not what men, but what they thought. A man should learn to detect and watch that gleam of light which flashes across his mind from within, more than the lustre of the firmament of bards and sages. Yet he dismisses without notice his thought, because it is his. In every work of genius we recognize our own rejected thoughts; they come back to us with a certain alienated majesty. Great works of art have no more affecting lesson for us than this. They teach us to abide by our spontaneous impression with good-humored inflexibility then most when the whole cry of voices is on the other side. Else to-morrow a stranger will say with masterly good sense precisely what we have thought and felt all the time, and we shall be forced to take with shame our own opinion from another.

There is a time in every man's education when he arrives at the conviction that envy is ignorance; that imitation is suicide; that he must take himself for better for worse as his portion; that though the wide universe is full of good, no kernel of nourishing corn can come to him but through his toil bestowed on that plot of ground which is given to him to till. The power which resides in him is new in nature, and none but he knows what that is which he can do, nor does he know until he has tried. Not for nothing one face, one character, one fact, makes much impression on him, and another none. It is not without preestablished harmony, this sculpture in the memory. The eye was placed where one ray should fall, that it might testify of that particular ray. Bravely let him speak the utmost syllable of his confession. We but half express ourselves, and are ashamed of that divine idea which each of us represents. It may be safely trusted as proportionate and of good issues, so it be faithfully imparted, but God will not have his work made manifest by cowards. It needs a divine man to exhibit anything divine. A man is relieved and gay when he has put his heart into his work and done his best; but what he has said or done otherwise shall give him no peace. It is a deliverance which does not deliver. In the attempt his genius deserts him; no muse befriends; no invention, no hope.

Trust thyself: every heart vibrates to that iron string. Accept the place the divine providence has found for you, the society of your contemporaries, the connection of events. Great men have always done so, and confided themselves childlike to the genius of their age, betraying their perception that the Eternal was stirring at their heart, working through their hands, predominating in all their being. And we are now men, and must accept in the highest mind the same transcendent destiny; and not pinched in a corner, not cowards fleeing before a revolution, but redeemers and benefactors, pious aspirants to be noble clay under the Almighty effort let us advance on Chaos and the Dark.

What pretty oracles nature yields us on this text in the face and behavior of children, babes, and even brutes. That divided and rebel mind, that distrust of a sentiment because our arithmetic has computed the strength and means opposed to our purpose, these have not. Their mind being whole, their eye is as yet unconquered, and when we look in their faces, we are disconcerted. Infancy conforms to nobody; all conform to it; so that one babe commonly makes four or five out of the adults who prattle and play to it. So God has armed youth and puberty and manhood no less with its own piquancy and charm, and made it enviable and gracious and its claims not to be put by, it will stand by itself. Do not think the youth has no force, because he cannot speak to you and me. Hark! in the next room who spoke so clear and emphatic? It seems he knows how to speak to his contemporaries. Good Heaven! it is he! it is that very lump of bashfulness and phlegm which for weeks has done nothing but eat when you were by, and now rolls out these words like bellstrokes. It seems he knows how to speak to his contemporaries. Good Heaven! It is he! It is that very lump of bashfulness and phlegm which for weeks has done nothing but eat when you were by, and now rolls out these words like bell-strokes. It seems he knows how to speak to his contemporaries. Bashful or bold then, he will know how to make us seniors very unnecessary.

The nonchalance of boys who are sure of a dinner, and would disdain as much as a lord to do or say aught to conciliate one, is the healthy attitude of human nature. How is a boy the master of society; independent, irresponsible, looking out from his corner on such people and facts as pass by, he tries and sentences them on their merits, in the swift, summary way of boys, as good, bad, interesting, silly, eloquent, troublesome. He cumbers himself never about consequences, about interests; he gives an independent, genuine verdict. You must court him; he does not court you. But the man is as it were clapped into jail by his consciousness. As soon as he has once acted or spoken with eclat he is a committed person, watched by the sympathy or the hatred of hundreds, whose affections must now enter into his account. There is no Lethe[†] for this. Ah, that he could pass again into his neutral, godlike independence! Who can thus lose all pledge and, having observed, observe again from the same unaffected, unbiased, unbribable, unaffrighted innocence, must always be formidable, must always engage the poet's and the man's regards. Of such an immortal youth the force would be felt. He would utter opinions on all passing affairs, which being seen to be not private but necessary, would sink like darts into the ear of men and put them in fear.

These are the voices which we hear in solitude, but they grow faint and inaudible as we enter into the world. Society everywhere is in conspiracy against the manhood of every one of its members. Society is a joint-stock company,[†] in which the members agree, for the better securing of his bread to each shareholder, to surrender the liberty and culture of the eater. The virtue in most request is conformity. Self-reliance is its aversion. It loves not realities and creators, but names and customs.

Whoso would be a man, must be a nonconformist. He who would gather immortal palms must not be hindered by the name of goodness, but must explore if it be goodness. Nothing is at last sacred but the integrity of our own mind. Absolve you to yourself, and you shall have the suffrage of the world. I remember an answer which when quite young I was prompted to make to a valued adviser who was wont to importune me with the dear old doctrines of the church. On my saying, What have I to do with the sacredness of traditions, if I live wholly from within? my friend suggested,—"But these impulses may be from below, not from above." I replied, "They do not seem to me to be such; but if I am the devil's child, I will live then from the devil." No law can be sacred to me but that of my nature. Good and bad are but names very readily transferable to that or this; the only right is what is after my constitution; the only wrong what is against it. A man is to carry himself in the presence of all opposition as if every thing were titular and ephemeral but he. I am ashamed to think how easily we capitulate to badges and names, to large societies and dead institutions. Every decent and well-spoken individual affects and sways me more than is right. I ought to go upright and vital, and speak the rude truth in all ways. If malice and vanity wear the coat of philanthropy, shall that pass? If an angry bigot assumes this bountiful cause of Abolition, and comes to me with his last news from Barbadoes,[†] why should I not say to him, "Go love thy infant; love thy wood-chopper; be good-natured and modest; have that grace; and never varnish your hard, uncharitable ambition with this incredible tenderness for black folk a thousand miles off. Thy love afar is spite at home." Rough and graceless would be such greeting, but truth is handsomer than the affectation of love. Your goodness must have some edge to it,—else it is none. The doctrine of hatred must be preached, as the counteraction of the doctrine of love, when that pules and whines. I shun father and mother and wife and brother when my genius[†] calls me. I would write on the lintels of the doorpost, *Whim*. I hope it is somewhat better than whim at last, but we cannot spend the day in explanation. Expect me not to show cause why I seek or why I exclude company. Then, again, do not tell me, as a good man did today, of my obligation to put all poor men in good situations. Are they my poor? I tell thee, thou foolish philanthropist, that I grudge the dollar, the dime, the cent I give to such men as do not belong to me and to whom I do not belong. There is a class of persons to whom by all spiritual affinity I am bought and sold; for them I will go to prison if need be; but your miscellaneous popular charities; the education at college of fools; the building of meeting-houses to the vain end to which many now stand; alms to sots, and the thousandfold Relief Societies;[†]—though I confess with shame I sometimes succumb and give the dollar, it is a wicked dollar, which by-and-by I shall have the manhood to withhold.

Virtues are, in the popular estimate, rather the exception than the rule. There is the man *and* his virtues. Men do what is called a good action, as some piece of courage or charity, much as they would pay a fine in expiation of daily non-appearance on parade. Their works are done as an apology or extenuation of their living in the world,—as invalids and the insane pay a high board. Their virtues are penances. I do not wish to expiate, but to live. My life is not an apology, but a life. It is for itself and not for a spectacle. I much prefer that it should be of a lower strain, so it be genuine and equal, than that it should be glittering and unsteady. I wish it to be sound and sweet, and not to need diet and bleeding.† My life should be unique; it should be an alms, a battle, a conquest, a medicine. I ask primary evidence that you are a man, and refuse this appeal from the man to his actions. I know that for myself it makes no difference whether I do or forbear those actions which are reckoned excellent. I cannot consent to pay for a privilege where I have intrinsic right. Few and mean as my gifts may be, I actually am, and do not need for my own assurance or the assurance of my fellows any secondary testimony.

What I must do is all that concerns me, not what the people think. This rule, equally arduous in actual and in intellectual life, may serve for the whole distinction between greatness and meanness. It is the harder because you will always find those who think they know what is your duty better than you know it. It is easy in the world to live after the world's opinion; it is easy in solitude to live after our own; but the great man is he who in the midst of the crowd keeps with perfect sweetness the independence of solitude.

The objection to conforming to usages that have become dead to you is that it scatters your force. It loses your time and blurs the impression of your character. If you maintain a dead church, contribute to a dead Bible Society, vote with a great party either for the Government or against it, spread your table like base housekeepers,—under all these screens I have difficulty to detect the precise man you are. And of course so much force is withdrawn from your proper life. But do your thing, and I shall know you. Do your work, and you shall reinforce yourself. A man must consider what a blindman's-buff† is this game of conformity. If I know your sect I anticipate your argument. I hear a preacher announce for his text and topic the expediency of one of the institutions of his church. Do I not know beforehand that not possibly can he say a new and spontaneous word? Do I not know that with all this ostentation of examining the grounds of the institution he will do no such thing? Do I not know that he is pledged to himself not to look but at one side, the permitted side, not as a man, but as a parish minister? He is a retained attorney, and these airs of the bench are the emptiest affectation. Well, most men have bound their eyes with one or another handkerchief, and attached themselves to some one of these communities of opinion. This conformity makes them not false in a few particulars, authors of a few lies, but false in all particulars. Their every truth is not quite true. Their two is not the real two, their four not the real four: so that every word they say chagrins us and we know not where to begin to set them right. Meantime nature is not slow to equip us in the prison-uniform of the party to which we adhere. We come to wear one cut of face and figure, and acquire by degrees the gentlest asinine expression. There is a mortifying experience in particular, which does not fail to wreak itself also in the general history; I mean "the foolish face of praise," the forced smile which we put on in company where we do not feel at ease, in answer to conversation which does not interest us. The muscles, not spontaneously moved but moved by a low usurping wilfulness, grow tight about the outline of the face, and make the most disagreeable sensation; a sensation of rebuke and warning which no brave young man will suffer twice.

For non-conformity the world whips you with its displeasure. And therefore a man must know how to estimate a sour face. The bystanders look askance on him in the public street or in the friend's parlor. If this aversation had its origin in contempt and resistance like his own he might well go home with a sad countenance; but the sour faces of the multitude, like their sweet faces, have no deep cause—disguise no god, but are put on and off as the wind blows and a newspaper directs. Yet is the discontent of the multitude more formidable than that of the senate and the college. It is easy enough for a firm man who knows the world to brook the rage of the cultivated classes. Their rage is decorous and prudent, for they are timid, as being very vulnerable themselves. But when to their feminine rage the indignation of the people is added, when the ignorant and the poor are aroused, when the unintelligent brute force that lies at the bottom of society is made to growl and mow, it needs the habit of magnanimity and religion to treat it godlike as a trifle of no concernment.

The other terror that scares us from self-trust is our consistency; a reverence for our past act or word because the eyes of others have no other data for computing our orbit than our past acts, and we are loath to disappoint them.

But why should you keep your head over your shoulder? Why drag about this monstrous corpse of your memory, lest you contradict somewhat you have stated in this or that public place? Suppose you should contradict yourself; what then? It seems to be a rule of wisdom never to rely on your memory alone, scarcely even in acts of pure memory, but to bring the past for judgment into the thousand eyed present, and live ever in a new day. Trust your emotion. In your metaphysics you have denied personality to the Deity, yet when the devout motions of the soul come, yield to them heart and life, though they should clothe God with shape and color. Leave your theory, as Joseph his coat in the hand of the harlot,† and flee.

A foolish consistency is the hobgoblin of little minds, adored by little statesmen and philosophers and divines. With consistency a great soul has simply nothing to do. He may as well concern himself with his shadow on the wall. Out upon your guarded lips! Sew them up with packthread, do. Else if you would be a man speak what you think to-day in words as hard as cannon balls, and to-morrow speak what to-morrow thinks in hard words again, though it contradict every thing you said to-day. Ah, then, exclaim the aged ladies, you shall be sure to be misunderstood! Misunderstood! It is a right fool's word. Is it so bad then to be misunderstood? Pythagoras† was misunderstood, and Socrates,† and Jesus,† and Luther,† and Copernicus,† and Galileo,† and Newton,† and every pure and wise spirit that ever took flesh. To be great is to be misunderstood.

I suppose no man can violate his nature. All the sallies of his will are rounded in by the law of his being, as the inequalities of Andes† and Himmaleh† are insignificant in the curve of the sphere. Nor does it matter how you gauge and try him. A character is like an acrostic† or Alexandrian stanza;†—read it forward, backward, or across, it still spells the same thing. In this pleasing contrite wood-life which God allows me, let me record day by day my honest thought without prospect or retrospect, and I cannot doubt, it will be found symmetrical, though I mean it not and see it not. My book should smell of pines and resound with the hum of insects. The swallow over my window should interweave that thread or straw he carries in his bill into my web also. We pass for what we are. Character teaches above our wills. Men imagine that they communicate their virtue or vice only by overt actions, and do not see that virtue or vice emit a breath every moment.

Fear never but you shall be consistent in whatever variety of actions, so they be each honest and natural in their hour. For of one will, the actions will be harmonious, however unlike they seem. These varieties are lost sight of when seen at a little distance, at a little height of thought. One tendency unites them all. The voyage of the best ship is a zigzag line of a hundred tacks. This is only microscopic criticism. See the line from a sufficient distance, and it straightens itself to the average tendency. Your genuine action will explain itself and will explain your other genuine actions. Your conformity explains nothing. Act singly, and what you have already done singly will justify you now. Greatness always appeals to the future. If I can be great enough now to do right and scorn eyes, I must have done so much right before as to defend me now. Be it how it will, do right now. Always scorn appearances and you always may. The force of character is cumulative. All the foregone days of virtue work their health into this. What makes the majesty of the heroes of the senate and the field, which so fills the imagination? The consciousness of a train of great days and victories behind. There they all stand and shed an united light on the advancing actor. He is attended as by a visible escort of angels to every man's eye. That is it which throws thunder into Chatham's voice,† and dignity into Washington's port, and America into Adams's† eye. Honor is venerable to us because it is no ephemeris. It is always ancient virtue. We worship it to-day because it is not of to-day. We love it and pay it homage because it is not a trap for our love and homage, but is self-dependent, self-derived, and therefore of an old immaculate pedigree, even if shown in a young person.

I hope in these days we have heard the last of conformity and consistency. Let the words be gazetted and ridiculous henceforward. Instead of the gong for dinner, let us hear a whistle from the Spartan fife.† Let us bow and apologize never more. A great man is coming to eat at my house. I do not wish to please him: I wish that he should wish to please me. I will stand here for humanity, and though I would make it kind, I would make it true. Let us affront and reprimand the smooth mediocrity and squalid contentment of the times, and hurl in the face of custom and trade and office, the fact which is the upshot of all history, that there is a great responsible Thinker and Actor moving wherever moves a man; that a true man belongs to no other time or place, but is the centre of things. Where he is, there is nature. He measures you and all men and all events. You are constrained to accept his standard. Ordinarily, every body in society reminds us of somewhat else, or of some other person. Character, reality, reminds you of nothing else; it takes place of the whole creation. The man must be so much that he must make all circumstances indifferent—put all means into the shade. This all great men are and do. Every true man is a cause, a country, and an age; requires infinite spaces and numbers and time fully to accomplish his thought;—and posterity seem to follow his steps as a procession. A man Cæsar† is born, and for ages after we have a Roman Empire. Christ is born, and millions of minds so grow and cleave to his genius that he is confounded with virtue and the possible of man. An institution is the lengthened shadow of one man; as, the Reformation, of Luther;† Quakerism, of Fox;† Methodism, of Wesley;† Abolition, of Clarkson.† Scipio,† Milton called "the height of Rome"; and all history resolves itself very easily into the biography of a few stout and earnest persons.

Let a man then know his worth, and keep things under his feet. Let him not peep or steal, or skulk up and down with the air of a charity-boy,† a bastard, or an interloper in the world which exists for him. But the man in the street, finding no worth in himself which corresponds to the force which built a tower or sculptured a marble god, feels poor when he looks at these. To him a palace, a statue, or a costly book have an alien and forbidding air, much like a gay equipage, and seem to say like that, 'Who are you, sir?' Yet they all are his, suitors for his notice, petitioners to his faculties that they will come out and take possession. The picture waits for my verdict; it is not to command me, but I am to settle its claim to praise. That popular fable of the sot who was picked up dead drunk in the street, carried to the duke's house, washed and dressed and laid in the duke's bed, and, on his waking, treated with all obsequious ceremony like the duke, and assured that he had been insane—owes its popularity to the fact that it symbolizes so well the state of man, who is in the world a sort of sot, but now and then wakes up, exercises his reason and finds himself a true prince.

Our reading is mendicant and sycophantic. In history our imagination makes fools of us, plays us false. Kingdom and lordship, power and estate, are a gaudier vocabulary than private John and Edward in a small house and common day's work: but the things of life are the same to both: the sum total of both is the same. Why all this deference to Alfred† and Scanderbeg† and Gustavus?† Suppose they were virtuous; did they wear out virtue? As great a stake depends on your private act to-day as followed their public and renowned steps. When private men shall act with original views, the lustre will be transferred from the actions of kings to those of gentlemen.

The world has indeed been instructed by its kings, who have so magnetized the eyes of nations. It has been taught by this colossal symbol the mutual reverence that is due from man to man. The joyful loyalty with which men have everywhere suffered the king, the noble, or the great proprietor to walk among them by a law of his own, make his own scale of men and things and reverse theirs, pay for benefits not with money but with honor, and represent the Law in his person, was the hieroglyphic by which they obscurely signified their consciousness of their own right and comeliness, the right of every man.

The magnetism which all original action exerts is explained when we inquire the reason of self-trust. Who is the Trustee? What is the aboriginal Self, on which a universal reliance may be grounded? What is the nature and power of that science-baffling star, without parallax, without calculable elements, which shoots a ray of beauty even into trivial and impure actions, if the least mark of independence appear? The inquiry leads us to that source, at once the essence of genius, the essence of virtue, and the essence of life, which we call Spontaneity or Instinct. We denote this primary wisdom as Intuition, whilst all later teachings are tuitions. In that deep force, the last fact behind which analysis cannot go, all things find their common origin. For the sense of being which in calm hours rises, we know not how, in the soul, is not diverse from things, from space from light, from time, from man, but one with them and proceedeth obviously from the same source whence their life and being also proceedeth. We first share the life by which things exist and afterwards see them as appearances in nature and forget that we have shared their cause. Here is the fountain of action and the fountain of thought. Here are the lungs of that inspiration which giveth man wisdom, of that inspiration of man which cannot be denied without impiety and atheism. We lie in the lap of immense intelligence, which makes us organs of its activity and receivers of its truth. When we discern justice, when we discern truth, we do nothing of ourselves, but allow a passage to its beams. If we ask whence this comes, if we seek to pry into the soul that causes—all metaphysics, all philosophy is at fault. Its presence or its absence is all we can affirm. Every man discerns between the voluntary acts of his mind and his involuntary perceptions. And to his involuntary perceptions he knows a perfect respect is due. He may err in the expression of them, but he knows that these things are so, like day and night, not to be disputed. All my wilful actions and acquisitions are but roving;—the most trivial reverie, the faintest native emotion, are domestic and divine. Thoughtless people contradict as readily the statement of perceptions as of opinions, or rather much more readily; for they do not distinguish between perception and notion. They fancy that I choose to see this or that thing. But perception is not whimsical, but fatal. If I see a trait, my children will see it after me, and in course of time all mankind,—although it may chance that no one has seen it before me. For my perception of it is as much a fact as the sun.

The relations of the soul to the divine spirit are so pure that it is profane to seek to interpose helps. It must be that when God speaketh he should communicate, not one thing, but all things; should fill the world with his voice; should scatter forth light, nature, time, souls, from the centre of the present thought; and new date and new create the whole. Whenever a mind is simple and receives a divine wisdom, then old things pass away,—means, teachers, texts, temples fall; it lives now, and absorbs past and future into the present hour. All things are made sacred by relation to it,—one thing as much as another. All things are dissolved to their centre by their cause, and in the universal miracle petty and particular miracles disappear. This is and must be. If therefore a man claims to know and speak of God and carries you backward to the phraseology of some old mouldered nation in another country, in another world, believe him not. Is the acorn better than the oak which is its fulness and completion? Is the parent better than the child into whom he has cast his ripened being? Whence then this worship of the past? The centuries are conspirators against the sanity and majesty of the soul. Time and space are but physiological colors which the eye maketh, but the soul is light; where it is, is day; where it was, is night; and history is an impertinence and an injury if it be any thing more than a cheerful apologue or parable of my being and becoming.

Man is timid and apologetic; he is no longer upright; he dares not say "I think," "I am,"[†] but quotes some saint or sage. He is ashamed before the blade of grass or the blowing rose. These roses under my window make no reference to former roses or to better ones; they are for what they are; they exist with God to-day. There is no time to them. There is simply the rose; it is perfect in every moment of its existence. Before a leaf-bud has burst, its whole life acts; in the fullblown flower there is no more; in the leafless root there is no less. Its nature is satisfied and it satisfies nature in all moments alike. There is no time to it. But man postpones or remembers; he does not live in the present, but with reverted eye laments the past, or, heedless of the riches that surround him, stands on tiptoe to foresee the future. He cannot be happy and strong until he too lives with nature in the present, above time.

This should be plain enough. Yet see what strong intellects dare not yet hear God himself unless he speak the phraseology of I know not what David,† or Jeremiah,† or Paul.† We shall not always set so great a price on a few texts, on a few lives. We are like children who repeat by rote the sentences of grandames and tutors, and, as they grow older, of the men of talents and character they chance to see,—painfully recollecting the exact words they spoke; afterwards, when they come into the point of view which those had who uttered these sayings, they understand them and are willing to let the words go; for at any time they can use words as good when occasion comes. So was it with us, so will it be, if we proceed. If we live truly, we shall see truly. It is as easy for the strong man to be strong, as it is for the weak to be weak. When we have new perception, we shall gladly disburthen the memory of its hoarded treasures as old rubbish. When a man lives with God, his voice shall be as sweet as the murmur of the brook and the rustle of the corn.

And now at last the highest truth on this subject remains unsaid; probably cannot be said; for all that we say is the far off remembering of the intuition. That thought, by what I can now nearest approach to say it, is this. When good is near you, when you have life in yourself,—it is not by any known or appointed way; you shall not discern the footprints of any other; you shall not see the face of man; you shall not hear any name;—the way, the thought, the good, shall be wholly strange and new. It shall exclude all other being. You take the way from man, not to man. All persons that ever existed are its fugitive ministers. There shall be no fear in it. Fear and hope are alike beneath it. It asks nothing. There is somewhat low even in hope. We are then in vision. There is nothing that can be called gratitude, nor properly joy. The soul is raised over passion. It seeth identity and eternal causation. It is a perceiving that Truth and Right are. Hence it becomes a Tranquillity out of the knowing that all things go well. Vast spaces of nature; the Atlantic Ocean, the South Sea; vast intervals of time, years, centuries, are of no account. This which I think and feel underlay that former state of life and circumstances, as it does underlie my present and will always all circumstances, and what is called life and what is called death.

Life only avails, not the having lived. Power ceases in the instant of repose; it resides in the moment of transition from a past to a new state, in the shooting of the gulf, in the darting to an aim. This one fact the world hates, that the soul *becomes;* for that forever degrades the past; turns all riches to poverty, all reputation to a shame; confounds the saint with the rogue; shoves Jesus and Judas† equally aside. Why then do we prate of self-reliance? Inasmuch as the soul is present there will be power not confident but agent. To talk of reliance is a poor external way of speaking. Speak rather of that which relies because it works and is. Who has more soul than I masters me, though he should not raise his finger. Round him I must revolve by the gravitation of spirits. Who has less I rule with like facility. We fancy it rhetoric when we speak of eminent virtue. We do not yet see that virtue is Height, and that a man or a company of men, plastic and permeable to principles, by the law of nature must overpower and ride all cities, nations, kings, rich men, poets, who are not.

This is the ultimate fact which we so quickly reach on this, as on every topic, the resolution of all into the ever-blessed ONE. Virtue is the governor, the creator, the reality. All things real are so by so much virtue as they contain. Hardship, husbandry, hunting, whaling, war, eloquence, personal weight, are somewhat, and engage my respect as examples of the soul's presence and impure action. I see the same law working in nature for conservation and growth. The poise of a planet, the bended tree recovering itself from the strong wind, the vital resources of every animal and vegetable, are also demonstrations of the self-sufficing and therefore self-relying soul. All history, from its highest to its trivial passages, is the various record of this power.

Thus all concentrates; let us not rove; let us sit at home with the cause. Let us stun and astonish the intruding rabble of men and books and institutions by a simple declaration of the divine fact. Bid them take the shoes from off their feet, for God is here within. Let our simplicity judge them, and our docility to our own law demonstrate the poverty of nature and fortune beside our native riches.

But now we are a mob. Man does not stand in awe of man, nor is the soul admonished to stay at home, to put itself in communication with the internal ocean, but it goes abroad to beg a cup of water of the urns of men. We must go alone. Isolation must precede true society. I like the silent church before the service begins, better than any preaching. How far off, how cool, how chaste the persons look, begirt each one with a precinct or sanctuary. Se let us always sit. Why should we assume the faults of our friend, or wife, or father, or child, because they sit around our hearth, or are said to have the same blood? All men have my blood and I have all men's. Not for that will I adopt their petulance or folly, even to the extent of being ashamed of it. But your isolation must not be mechanical, but spiritual, that is, must be elevation.

At times the whole world seems to be in conspiracy to importune you with emphatic trifles. Friend, client, child, sickness, fear, want, charity, all knock at once at thy closet door and say, "Come out unto us."—Do not spill thy soul; do not all descend; keep thy state; stay at home in thine own heaven; come not for a moment into their facts, into their hubbub of conflicting appearances, but let in the light of thy law on their confusion. The power men possess to annoy me I give them by a weak curiosity. No man can come near me but through my act. "What we love that we have, but by desire we bereave ourselves of the love."

If we cannot at once rise to the sanctities of obedience and faith, let us at least resist our temptations, let us enter into the state of war and wake Thor and Woden,† courage and constancy, in our Saxon† breasts. This is to be done in our smooth times by speaking the truth. Check this lying hospitality and lying affection. Live no longer to the expectation of these deceived and deceiving people with whom we converse. Say to them, O father, O mother, O wife, O brother, O friend, I have lived with you after appearances hitherto. Henceforward I am the truth's. Be it known unto you that henceforward I obey no law less than the eternal law. I will have no covenants but proximities. I shall endeavor to nourish my parents, to support my family, to be the chaste husband of one wife,—but these relations I must fill after a new and unprecedented way. I appeal from your customs. I must be myself. I cannot break myself any longer for you, or you. If you can love me for what I am, we shall be happier. If you cannot, I will still seek to deserve that you should. I must be myself. I will not hide my tastes or aversions. I will so trust that what is deep is holy, that I will do strongly before the sun and moon whatever inly rejoices me and the heart appoints. If you are noble, I will love you; if you are not, I will not hurt you and myself by hypocritical attentions. If you are true, but not in the same truth with me, cleave to your companions; I will seek my own. I do this not selfishly but humbly and truly. It is alike your interest, and mine, and all men's, however long we have dwelt in lies, to live in truth. Does this sound harsh to-day? You will soon love what is dictated by your nature as well as mine, and if we follow the truth it will bring us out safe at last.—But so may you give these friends pain. Yes, but I cannot sell my liberty and my power, to save their sensibility. Besides, all persons have their moments of reason, when they look out into the region of absolute truth; then will they justify me and do the same thing.

The populace think that your rejection of popular standards is a rejection of all standard, and mere antinomianism;† and the bold sensualist will use the name of philosophy to gild his crimes. But the law of consciousness abides. There are two confessionals, in one or the other of which we must be shriven. You may fulfil your round of duties by clearing yourself in the *direct,* or in the *reflex* way. Consider whether you have satisfied your relations to father, mother, cousin, neighbor, town, cat and dog; whether any of these can upbraid you. But I may also neglect this reflex standard and absolve me to myself. I have my own stern claims and perfect circle. It denies the name of duty to many offices that are called duties. But if I can discharge its debts it enables me to dispense with the popular code. If any one imagines that this law is lax, let him keep its commandment one day.

And truly it demands something godlike in him who has cast off the common motives of humanity and has ventured to trust himself for a task-master. High be his heart, faithful his will, clear his sight, that he may in good earnest be doctrine, society, law, to himself, that a simple purpose may be to him as strong as iron necessity is to others.

If any man consider the present aspects of what is called by distinction *society,* he will see the need of these ethics, The sinew and heart of man seem to be drawn out, and we are become timorous desponding whimperers. We are afraid of truth, afraid of fortune, afraid of death, and afraid of each other. Our age yields no great and perfect persons. We want men and women who shall renovate life and our social state, but we see that most natures are insolvent; cannot satisfy their own wants, have an ambition out of all proportion to their practical force, and so do lean and beg day and night continually. Our housekeeping is mendicant, our arts, our occupations, our marriages, our religion we have not chosen, but society has chosen for us. We are parlor soldiers. The rugged battle of fate, where strength is born, we shun.

If our young men miscarry in their first enterprises they lose all heart. If the young merchant fails, men say he is ruined. If the finest genius studies at one of our colleges, and is not installed in an office within one year afterwards, in the cities or suburbs of Boston or New York, it seems to his friends and to himself that he is right in being disheartened and in complaining the rest of his life. A sturdy lad from New Hamsphire or Vermont, who in turn tries all the professions, who *teams it, farms it, peddles,* keeps a school, preaches, edits a newspaper, goes to Congress, buys a township, and so forth, in successive years, and always like a cat falls on his feet, is worth a hundred of these city dolls. He walks abreast with his days and feels no shame in not "studying a profession," for he does not postpone his life, but lives already. He has not one chance, but a hundred chances. Let a stoic† arise who shall reveal the resources of man and tell men they are not leaning willows, but can and must detach themselves; that with the exercise of self-trust, new powers shall appear; that a man is the word made flesh, born to shed healing to the nations, that he should be ashamed of our compassion, and that the moment he acts from himself, tossing the laws, the books, idolatries and customs out of the window,—we pity him no more but thank and revere him;—and that teacher shall restore the life of man to splendor and make his name dear to all History.

It is easy to see that a greater self-reliance—a new respect for the divinity in man—must work a revolution in all the offices and relations of men; in their religion; in their education; in their pursuits; their modes of living; their association; in their property; in their speculative views.

1. In what prayers do men allow themselves! That which they call a holy office is not so much as brave and manly. Prayer looks abroad and asks for some foreign addition to come through some foreign virtue, and loses itself in endless mazes of natural and supernatural, and mediatorial and miraculous. Prayer that craves a particular commodity—anything less than all good, is vicious. Prayer is the contemplation of the facts of life from the highest point of view. It is the soliloquy of a beholding and jubilant soul. It is the spirit of God pronouncing his works good. But prayer as a means to effect a private end is theft and meanness. It supposes dualism and not unity in nature and consciousness. As soon as the man is at one with God, he will not beg. He will then see prayer in all action. The prayer of the farmer kneeling in his field to weed it, the prayer of the rower kneeling with the stroke of his oar, are true prayers heard throughout nature, though for cheap ends. Caratach, in Fletcher's Bonduca,† when admonished to inquire the mind of the god Audate, replies:

> His hidden meaning lies in our endeavors;
> Our valors are our best gods.

Another sort of false prayers are our regrets. Discontent is the want of self-reliance: it is infirmity of will. Regret calamities if you can thereby help the sufferer; if not, attend your own work and already the evil begins to be repaired. Our sympathy is just as base. We come to them who weep foolishly and sit down and cry for company, instead of imparting to them truth and health in rough electric shocks, putting them once more in communication with the soul. The secret of fortune is joy in our hands. Welcome evermore to gods and men is the self-helping man. For him all doors are flung wide. Him all tongues greet, all honors crown, all eyes follow with desire. Our love goes out to him and embraces him because he did not need it. We solicitously and apologetically caress and celebrate him because he held on his way and scorned our disapprobation. The gods love him because men hated him. "To the persevering mortal," said Zoroaster,† "the blessed Immortals are swift."

As men's prayers are a disease of the will, so are their creeds a disease of the intellect. They say with those foolish Israelites, "Let not God speak to us, lest we die. Speak thou, speak any man with us, and we will obey." Everywhere I am bereaved of meeting God in my brother, because he has shut his own temple doors and recites fables merely of his brother's, or his brother's brother's God. Every new mind is a new classification. If it prove a mind of uncommon activity and power, a Locke,† a Lavoisier,† a Hutton,† a Bentham,† a Spurzheim,† it imposes its classification on other men, and lo! a new system. In proportion always to the depth of the thought, and so to the number of the objects it touches and brings within reach of the pupil, is his complacency. But chiefly is this apparent in creeds and churches, which are also classifications of some powerful mind acting on the great elemental thought of Duty and man's relation to the Highest. Such is Calvinism,† Quakerism,† Swedenborgism.† The pupil takes the same delight in subordinating every thing to the new terminology that a girl does who has just learned botany in seeing a new earth and new seasons thereby. It will happen for a time that the pupil will feel a real debt to the teacher—will find his intellectual power has grown by the study of his writings. This will continue until he has exhausted his master's mind. But in all unbalanced minds the classification is idolized, passes for the end and not for a speedily exhaustible means, so that the walls of the system blend to their eye in the remote horizon with the walls of the universe; the luminaries of heaven seem to them hung on the arch their master built. They cannot imagine how you aliens have any right to see—how you can see: "It must be somehow that you stole the light from us." They do not yet perceive that light, unsystematic, indomitable, will break into any cabin, even into theirs. Let them chirp awhile and call it their own. If they are honest and do well, presently their neat new pinfold will be too strait and low, will crack, will lean, will rot and vanish, and the immortal light, all young and joyful, million-orbed, million-colored, will beam over the universe as on the first morning.

2. It is for want of self-culture that the idol of Travelling, the idol of Italy, of England, of Egypt, remains for all educated Americans. They who made England, Italy, or Greece venerable in the imagination, did so not by rambling round creation as a moth round a lamp, but by sticking fast where they were, like an axis of the earth. In manly hours we feel that duty is our place and that the merry men of circumstance should follow as they may. The soul is no traveller: the wise man stays at home with the soul, and when his necessities, his duties, on any occasion call him from his house, or into foreign lands, he is at home still and is not gadding abroad from himself, and shall make men sensible by the expression of his countenance that he goes, the missionary of wisdom and virtue, and visits cities and men like a sovereign and not like an interloper or a valet.

I have no churlish objection to the circumnavigation of the globe for the purposes of art, of study, and benevolence, so that the man is first domesticated, or does not go abroad with the hope of finding somewhat greater than he knows. He who travels to be amused or to get somewhat which he does not carry, travels away from himself, and grows old even in youth among old things. In Thebes,† in Palmyra,† his will and mind have become old and dilapidated as they. He carries ruins to ruins.

Travelling is a fool's paradise. We owe to our first journeys the discovery that place is nothing. At home I dream that at Naples, at Rome, I can be intoxicated with beauty and lose my sadness. I pack my trunk, embrace my friends, embark on the sea and at last wake up in Naples, and there beside me is the stern Fact, the sad self, unrelenting, identical, that I fled from. I seek the Vatican† and the palaces. I affect to be intoxicated with sights and suggestions, but I am not intoxicated. My giant goes with me wherever I go.

3. But the rage of travelling is itself only a symptom of a deeper unsoundness affecting the whole intellectual action. The intellect is vagabond, and the universal system of education fosters restlessness. Our minds travel when our bodies are forced to stay at home. We imitate; and what is imitation but the travelling of the mind? Our houses are built with foreign taste; our shelves are garnished with foreign ornaments; our opinions, our tastes, our whole minds, lean, and follow the Past and the Distant, as the eyes of a maid follow her mistress. The soul created the arts wherever they have flourished. It was in his own mind that the artist sought his model. It was an application of his own thought to the thing to be done and the conditions to be observed. And why need we copy the Doric† or the Gothic† model? Beauty, convenience, grandeur of thought and quaint expression are as near to us to any, and if the American artist will study with hope and love the precise thing to be done by him, considering the climate, the soil, the length of the day, the wants of the people, the habit and form of the government, he will create a house in which all these will find themselves fitted, and taste and sentiment will be satisfied also.

Insist on yourself; never imitate. Your own gift you can present every moment with the cumulative force of a whole life's cultivation; but of the adopted talent of another you have only an extemporaneous half possession. That which each can do best, none but his Maker can teach him. No man yet knows what it is, nor can, till that person has exhibited it. Where is the master who could have taught Shakspeare?† Where is the master who could have instructed Franklin,† or Washington,† or Bacon,† or Newton? Every great man is an unique. The Scipionism of Scipio is precisely that part he could not borrow. If anybody will tell me whom the great man imitates in the original crisis when he performs a great act, I will tell him who else than himself can teach him. Shakspeare will never be made by the study of Shakspeare. Do that which is assigned thee and thou canst not hope too much or dare too much. There is at this moment, there is for me an utterance bare and grand as that of the colossal chisel of Phidias,† or trowel of the Egyptians, or the pen of Moses or Dante,† but different from all these. Not possibly will the soul, all rich, all eloquent, with thousand-cloven tongue, deign to repeat itself; but if I can hear what these patriarchs say, surely I can reply to them in the same pitch of voice; for the ear and the tongue are two organs of one nature. Dwell up there in the simple and noble regions of thy life, obey thy heart and thou shalt reproduce the Foreworld again.

4. As our Religion, our Education, our Art look abroad, so does our spirit of society. All men plume themselves on the improvement of society, and no man improves.

Society never advances. It recedes as fast on one side as it gains on the other. Its progress is only apparent like the workers of a treadmill. It undergoes continual changes; it is barbarous, it is civilized, it is christianized, it is rich, it is scientific; but this change is not amelioration. For every thing that is given something is taken. Society acquires new arts and loses old instincts. What a contrast between the well-clad, reading, writing, thinking American, with a watch, a pencil and a bill of exchange in his pocket, and the naked New Zealander, whose property is a club, a spear, a mat and an undivided twentieth of a shed to sleep under. But compare the health of the two men and you see that his aboriginal strength, the white man has lost. If the traveller tell us truly, strike the savage with a broad axe and in a day or two the flesh shall unite and heal as if you struck the blow into soft pitch, and the same blow shall send the white man to his grave.

The civilized man has built a coach, but has lost the use of his feet. He is supported on crutches, but lacks so much support of muscle. He has got a fine Geneva watch, but he has lost the skill to tell the hour by the sun. A Greenwich nautical almanac he has, and so being sure of the information when he wants it, the man in the street does not know a star in the sky. The solstice he does not observe; the equinox he knows as little; and the whole bright calendar of the year is without a dial in his mind. His note-books impair his memory: his libraries overload his wit; the insurance-office increases the number of accidents; and it may be a question whether machinery does not encumber; whether we have not lost by refinement some energy, by a christianity entrenched in establishments and forms some vigor of wild virtue. For every stoic was a stoic; but in Christendom where is the Christian?

There is no more deviation in the moral standard than in the standard of height or bulk. No greater men are now than ever were. A singular equality may be observed between the great men of the first and of the last ages; nor can all the science, art, religion, and philosophy of the nineteenth century avail to educate greater men than Plutarch's† heroes, three or four and twenty centuries ago. Not in time is the race progressive. Phocion,† Socrates, Anaxagoras,† Diogenes,† are great men, but they leave no class. He who is really of their class will not be called by their name, but be wholly his own man, and in his turn the founder of a sect. The arts and inventions of each period are only its costume and do not invigorate men. The harm of the improved machinery may compensate its good. Hudson† and Behring† accomplished so much in their fishing-boats as to astonish Parry and Franklin,† whose equipment exhausted the resources of science and art. Galileo, with an opera-glass, discovered a more splendid series of facts than any one since. Columbus found the New World in an undecked boat. It is curious to see the periodical disuse and perishing of means and machinery which were introduced with loud laudation a few years or centuries before. The great genius returns to essential man. We reckoned the improvements of the art of war among the triumphs of science, and yet Napoleon† conquered Europe by the Bivouac, which consisted of falling back on naked valor and disencumbering it of all aids. The Emperor held it impossible to make a perfect army, says Las Cases,† "without abolishing our arms, magazines, commissaries and carriages, until, in imitation of the Roman custom, the soldier should receive his supply of corn, grind it in his hand-mill and bake his bread himself."

Society is a wave. The wave moves onward, but the water of which it is composed does not. The same particle does not rise from the valley to the ridge. Its unity is only phenomenal. The persons who make up a nation to-day, die, and their experience with them.

And so the reliance on Property, including the reliance on governments which protect it, is the want of self-reliance. Men have looked away from themselves and at things so long that they have come to esteem what they call the soul's progress, namely, the religious, learned and civil institutions as guards of property, and they deprecate assaults on these, because they feel them to be assaults on property. They measure their esteem of each other by what each has, and not by what each is. But a cultivated man becomes ashamed of his property, ashamed of what he has, out of new respect for his being. Especially he hates what he has if he sees that it is accidental,—came to him by inheritance, or gift, or crime; then he feels that it is not having; it does not belong to him, has no root in him, and merely lies there because no revolution or no robber takes it away. But that which a man is, does always by necessity acquire, and what the man acquires, is permanent and living property, which does not wait the beck of rulers, or mobs, or revolutions, or fire, or storm, or bankruptcies, but perpetually renews itself wherever the man is put. "Thy lot or portion of life," said the Caliph Ali,† "is seeking after thee; therefore be at rest from seeking after if." Our dependence on these foreign goods leads us to our slavish respect for numbers. The political parties meet in numerous conventions; the greater the concourse and with each new uproar of announcement, The delegation from Essex! The Democrats from New Hampshire! The Whigs† of Maine! the young patriot feels himself stronger than before by a new thousand of eyes and arms. In like manner the reformers summon conventions and vote and resolve in multitude. But not so O friends! will the God deign to enter and inhabit you, but by a method precisely the reverse. It is only as a man puts off from himself all external support and stands alone that I see him to be strong and to prevail. He is weaker by every recruit to his banner. Is not a man better than a town? Ask nothing of men, and, in the endless mutation, thou only firm column must presently appear the upholder of all that surrounds thee. He who knows that power is in the soul, that he is weak only because he has looked for good out of him and elsewhere, and, so perceiving, throws himself unhesitatingly on his thought, instantly rights himself, stands in the erect position, commands his limbs, works miracles; just as a man who stands on his feet is stronger than a man who stands on his head.

So use all that is called Fortune. Most men gamble with her, and gain all, and lose all, as her wheel rolls. But do thou leave as unlawful these winnings, and deal with Cause and Effect, the chancellors of God. In the Will work and acquire, and thou hast chained the wheel of Chance, and shalt always drag her after thee. A political victory, a rise of rents, the recovery of your sick or the return of your absent friend, or some other quite external event raises your spirits, and you think good days are preparing for you. Do not believe it. It can never be so. Nothing can bring you peace but yourself. Nothing can bring you peace but the triumph of principles.

Self-Reliance
Glossary

"Ne te quaesiveris extra." – [*Latin*] "Do not seek for things outside yourself." This maxim would be considered an essential part of the Transcendentalists' doctrine.

Honest Man's Fortune – Francis Beaumont (1584-1616), and John Fletcher (1579-1625), were English dramatists who collaborated on several plays. The Beaumont and Fletcher folios, published in 1647 and 1679, contain these works. *Honest Man's Fortune* is a play in the 1647 folio.

Last Judgment – In Christian doctrine, this phrase refers to the time when Jesus Christ will return to Earth and judge all people according to their deeds.

Moses – According to the Old Testament, Moses delivered the Israelites out of Egyptian slavery and brought the Ten Commandments down from Mount Sinai.

Plato – (ca. 428-348 B.C.), one of the greatest of the ancient Greek philosophers

Milton – John Milton (1608-1674), the English poet who wrote the epic poem *Paradise Lost*

Lethe – in Greek mythology, the river of forgetfulness, one of the five rivers that run through the underworld

joint-stock company – a company that allows people to buy stock in it; they are then able to share in profits and losses.

Barbadoes – an island in the Caribbean that was central to the slave trade

genius – To the ancient Romans, a *genius* was a guardian spirit that watched over a person or place.

Relief Societies – charitable organizations

bleeding – a common medical treatment in the nineteenth century; it sometimes involved leeches and was supposed to rid a sick person of toxins and infections.

blindman's buff – a child's game in which a blindfolded player tries to catch and identify the other players

Joseph his…harlot – In the Old Testament, Joseph, Jacob's son who went to Egypt, is falsely accused of rape by Pharaoh's wife ("the harlot"); she uses his coat (not the "coat of many colors," but one indicating his rank in Egyptian society) as evidence.

Pythagoras – (580-500 B.C.), an ancient Greek mathematician

Socrates – (496-399 B.C.), a Greek philosopher and teacher of Plato; his Socratic method is at the foundation of Western thought.

Jesus – according to Christian doctrine, God's son in human form; Christians believe that Jesus gave up His own life to save people from sin.

Luther – Martin Luther (1483-1546), was a German monk who started the Protestant Reformation.

Copernicus – Nicolaus Copernicus (1473-1543), was a Polish astronomer who proved that the Earth revolves around the sun.

Galileo – Galileo Galilei (1564-1642), an Italian mathematician and astronomer who made major contributions to scientific thought in Europe

Newton – Sir Isaac Newton (1642-1727), was an important English mathematician who discovered the Laws of Motion.

Andes – a mountain range in South America that stretches over 5,000 miles along the Pacific Coast

Himmaleh – the Himalayan mountain system, which is made up of 100 separate mountains, including Mt. Everest

acrostic – a poem in which the first, middle, or last letter of each line spells a word or phrase when it is read in sequence

Alexandrian stanza – a phrase that reads the same backwards and forwards; a palindrome

Chatham's voice – William Pitt (1708-1778), the First Earl of Chatham, supported the American colonists' desire for independence from Great Britain. He was the British secretary of state during the Seven Years' War and later became prime minister of Great Britain.

Adams – John Adams (1789-1797), served as the first vice president and second president of the United States.

Spartan fife – The Spartans were a warrior people who defeated Athens in the Peleponessian Wars; the fife is a small flute played when soldiers march to battle.

Cæsar – Julius Cæsar (ca. 100-44 B.C.), was a Roman emperor and military leader. He expanded the Roman Empire so far that it reached the Atlantic Ocean.

the Reformation, of Luther – Christians had conflicting beliefs over Church doctrine. Because of these divisions, Martin Luther, in 1517, issued *The 95 Theses,* declaring that Jesus was the way to salvation. The result split the Church into Protestants and Roman Catholics.

Quakerism, of Fox – Commonly known as Quakers, The Religious Society of Friends was founded by George Fox (1624-1691), in England during the 17th century. Fox was known for his unusual approach to Christian faith and belief in gender equality. The Quakers have a belief system that focuses on intuitive knowledge that is similar to Transcendentalism.

Methodism, of Wesley – Charles Wesley (1707-1788) and John Wesley (1703-1791), helped found Methodism, a denomination of Protestantism, during the 18th century in England; Methodists were concerned with social issues of the time, including the abolition of slavery.

Clarkson – Thomas Clarkson (1760-1846), was a British abolitionist.

Scipio – Scipio Africanus Major (236-183 B.C.), a Roman general and statesman of the Roman Republic; he is best known for defeating Hannibal of Carthage.

charity-boy – a boy who attends a school for impoverished children

Alfred – Alfred "The Great" (871-899), was the king of a southwest portion of England, then called West Saxony. He fought in battles against the Vikings.

Scanderbeg – an Albanian national hero; his actual name is George Castriota (1405 - 1468). Scanderbeg was a revolutionary leader and fought against the Turks.

Gustavus – Gustavus Eriksson (1496-1560) was the first king of modern Sweden and the founder of the Vasa dynasty.

"'I think,' 'I am,'" – a reference to René Descartes' (1596-1650) famous philosophical dictum, "I think, therefore, I am" (*cogito ergo sum*)

David – a reference to the second king of Israel; David, ("Beloved One") was a poet, musician, and author who wrote much of the book of Psalms. As a young shepherd, David defeated Goliath with a sling and stones.

Jeremiah – a prophet in the Old Testament

Paul – St. Paul the Apostle (ca. 10-67), also called "Apostle to the Gentiles," converted to Christianity when Christ revealed Himself in a vision while Paul was on the road to Damascus. Paul's writings are used as the foundation for most Christian beliefs.

Judas – Judas Iscariot was one of the Twelve Apostles. He betrayed Jesus by handing Him over to the Roman authorities.

Thor and Woden – According to Viking and Germanic mythology, Thor is the god of thunder; Woden (also known as Odin) is the chief of the gods. "Thursday" and "Wednesday" were named after them.

Saxon – a reference to the "Anglo-Saxons"

antinomianism – the belief that moral laws should be flexible and are not universal

stoic – Stoicism, introduced by Zeno of Citium around 301 B.C., was a popular philosopy among the elite members of the Greco-Roman Empire. A stoic practices self-control, fortitude, and detachment from strong emotions in order to improve spiritual well-being and inner peace.

Fletcher's Bonduca – John Fletcher (1579-1625), was a Jacobean playwright who rivaled Shakespeare. His historic play *Bonduca* is about a Celtic queen who leads a revolt against the Romans in 60 A.D.

Zoroaster – (Zarathustra), a Persian prophet who founded Zoroastrianism; his name means, "He of the golden light." This ancient religion is based on the idea that life is a struggle between the forces of good and evil. Traditional scholars believe that Zoroaster (the Greek version of his name) lived around 500 B.C. and studied with the Greek philosopher Pythogarus, but modern scholars are not sure of this.

Locke – John Locke (1623-1704), was an English philosopher who developed the theory that thought and knowledge are based on information that is received from the senses.

Lavoisier – Antoine Laurent Lavoisier (1743-1794), the French scientist who is regarded as the founder of modern chemistry

Hutton – James Hutton (1726-1797), a Scottish geologist who advanced theories about the earth's surface—geologic changes occur slowly and over long periods of time

Bentham – Jeremy Bentham (1748-1832), a British philosopher, jurist, and legal and social reformer; he is best known for advocating animal rights, liberalism, and utilitarianism, the theory that actions should be directed at achieving the greatest happiness for the greatest number of people.

Spurzheim – Dr. Johann Gaspar Spurzheim (1776-1832), a German physician credited with helping to popularize the belief that character and personality could be determined by feeling the shape and formation of a person's skull; other editions of *Self-Reliance* have "Fourier"—a reference to Francois Marie Fourier (1772-1837), a French social theorist, visionary, and mystic who influenced Transcendentalism—instead of Spurzheim as the last name in the list.

Calvinism – John Calvin (1509-1564), was an important theologian of the Protestant Reformation.

Quakerism – See earlier Note, "*Quakerism, of Fox.*

Swedenborgism – Emanuel Swedenborg (1688-1772), a Swedish philosopher, theologian, and Christian mystic; at age 56, he began experiencing visions from God and wrote about his experiences. The philosophy of Swedenborgism, which was founded on his beliefs, emphasizes the belief in faith and charity.

Thebes – an ancient Egyptian city

Palmyra – an ancient city in the Middle East

Vatican – Vatican City, located in Rome, is the governmental capital of the Catholic Church; it is headed by the Pope.

Doric – The Doric order is a part of the organizational systems of ancient Greek architecture; Doric columns are characterized by fluted pillars and square tops.

Gothic – Gothic architecture flourished during the late medieval period in Europe; it is characterized by pointed arches, ribbed vaults, and flying buttresses. This style is most visible in cathedrals, churches, and castles.

Shakespeare – William Shakespeare (1564-1616), an English playwright and poet; he is widely considered to be the greatest writer in the English language.

Franklin – a reference to Benjamin Franklin (1706-1790), the American scientist, inventor, writer, philosopher, and diplomat; he was one of the most influential figures who helped free the colonies from England.

Washington – George Washington (1732-1799), was the first president of the United States and is considered to be the father of the nation.

Bacon – Francis Bacon (1561-1626), an English statesman, philosopher, and essayist; his scientific theory, based on observation and experimentation, is now called the "inductive method."

Phidias – (ca. 480-430 B.C.), a Greek sculptor, painter, and architect

Dante – Dante Alighieri (1265-1321), was an Italian poet; he is best known for *The Divine Comedy,* considered the greatest work written in Italian.

Plutarch – Mestrius Plutarchus (ca. 46-120), was a Greek historian, essayist, and biographer. His works, especially *Parallel Lives*, were a source for many of the plays of Shakespeare.

Phocion – (ca. 402-318 B.C.), Known as "The Good," Phocion was an Athenian politician who believed that virtue was achieved through extreme frugality.

Anaxagoras – (ca. 500-428 B.C.), a Greek philosopher and astronomer, whose theories eventually paved the way for an understanding of atoms

Diogenes – Diogenes of Sinope (ca. 412-323 B.C.), also called "The Cynic," was a Greek philosopher who searched the world for an "honest man."

Hudson – Henry Hudson (ca. 1570-1611), an English sea explorer and navigator; the Hudson River (US) and Hudson Bay (Canada) are named after him.

Behring – Vitus Jonassen Bering (1681-1741), was a Danish explorer who sailed for the Russian Navy.

Parry and Franklin – Sir William Edward Parry (1790-1855), explored the Arctic Ocean. Sir John Franklin (1786-1847), was an Arctic explorer and a British Royal Navy officer; he mapped approximately two-thirds of the coastline of North America.

Napoleon – Napoleon Bonaparte (176-1821), is considered one of the greatest military strategists of all time. He was a general during the French Revolution, the ruler of France (1799-1804), and the Emperor of France between 1804 and 1814, including four months in 1815.

Las Cases – Emmanuel Las Cases (1766-1842) was a French historian who recorded Napoleon's last conversations.

Caliph Ali – (ca. 599-661), the fourth Caliph (leader) of the Muslim community; Shia (Shiite) Muslims and Sunni Muslims see his divinity differently, and these views originally caused the schism that has existed since approximately the seventh century.

Whigs – a U.S. political party that existed from 1833 to 1854; it eventually evolved into the Republican Party.

FRIENDSHIP †

WE HAVE A GREAT deal more kindness than is ever spoken. Maugre all the selfishness that chills like east winds the world, the whole human family is bathed with an element of love like a fine ether. How many persons we meet in houses, whom we scarcely speak to, whom yet we honor, and who honor us! How many we see in the street, or sit with in church, whom, though silently, we warmly rejoice to be with! Read the language of these wandering eye-beams. The heart knoweth.

The effect of the indulgence of this human affection is a certain cordial exhilaration. In poetry and in common speech the emotions of benevolence and complacency which are felt towards others are likened to the material effects of fire; so swift, or much more swift, more active, more cheering, are these fine inward irradiations. From the highest degree of passionate love to the lowest degree of goodwill, they make the sweetness of life.

Our intellectual and active powers increase with our affection. The scholar sits down to write, and all his years of meditation do not furnish him with one good thought or happy expression; but it is necessary to write a letter to a friend,—and forthwith troops of gentle thoughts invest themselves, on every hand, with chosen words. See, in any house where virtue and self-respect abide, the palpitation which the approach of a stranger causes. A commended stranger is expected and announced, and an uneasiness betwixt pleasure and pain invades all the hearts of a household. His arrival almost brings fear to the good hearts that would welcome him. The house is dusted, all things fly into their places, the old coat is exchanged for the new, and they must get up a dinner if they can. Of a commended stranger, only the good report is told by others, only the good and new is heard by us. He stands to us for humanity. He is what we wish. Having imagined and invested him, we ask how we should stand related in conversation and action with such a man, and are uneasy with fear. The same idea exalts conversation with him. We talk better than we are wont. We have the nimblest fancy, a richer memory, and our dumb devil has taken leave for the time. For long hours we can continue a series of sincere, graceful, rich communications, drawn from the oldest, secretest experience, so that they who sit by, of our own kinsfolk and acquaintance, shall feel a lively surprise at our unusual powers. But as soon as the stranger begins to intrude his partialities, his definitions, his defects, into the conversation, it is all over. He has heard the first, the last and best he will ever hear from us. He is no stranger now. Vulgarity, ignorance, misapprehension are old acquaintances. Now, when he comes, he may get the order, the dress and the dinner,—but the throbbing of the heart and the communications of the soul, no more.

Pleasant as these jets of affection which make a young world for me again. Delicious is a just and firm encounter of two, in a thought, in a feeling. How beautiful, on their approach to this beating heart, the steps and forms of the gifted and the true! The moment we indulge our affections, the earth is metamorphosed: there is no winter and no night: all tragedies, all ennuis vanish,—all duties even; nothing fills the proceeding eternity but the forms all radiant of beloved persons. Let the soul be assured that somewhere in the universe it should rejoin its friend, and it would be content and cheerful alone for a thousand years.

I awoke this morning with devout thanksgiving for my friends, the old and the new. Shall I not call God the Beautiful, who daily showeth himself so to me in his gifts? I chide society, I embrace solitude, and yet I am not so ungrateful as not to see the wise, the lovely and the noble-minded, as from time to time they pass my gate. Who hears me, who understands me, becomes mine,—a possession for all time. Nor is nature so poor but she gives me this joy several times, and thus we weave social threads of our own, a new web of relations; and, as many thoughts in succession substantiate themselves, we shall by-and-by stand in a new world of our own creation, and no longer strangers and pilgrims in a traditionary globe. My friends have come to me unsought. The great God gave them to me. By oldest right, by the divine affinity of virtue with itself, I find them, or rather not I, but the Deity in me and in them derides, and cancel the thick walls of individual character, relation, age, sex, circumstance, at which he usually connives, and now makes many one. High thanks I owe you, excellent lovers, who carry out the world for me to new and noble depths, and enlarge the meaning of all my thoughts. These are not stark and stiffened persons, but the new born poetry of God,—poetry without stop,—hymn, ode and epic, poetry still flowing and not yet caked in dead books with annotation and grammar, but Apollo† and the Muses† chanting still. Will these too separate themselves from me again, or some of them? I know not, but I fear it not; for my relation to them is so pure, that we hold by simple affinity, and the Genius of my life being thus social, the same affinity will exert its energy on whomsoever is as noble as these men and women, wherever I may be.

I confess to an extreme tenderness of nature on this point. It is almost dangerous to me to "crush the sweet poison of misused wine" of the affections. A new person is to me always a great event and hinders me from sleep. I have often had fine fancies lately about two or three persons which have given me delicious hours; but the joy ends in the day; it yields no fruit. Thought is not born of it; my action is very little modified. I must feel pride in my friend's accomplishments as if they were mine,—wild, delicate, throbbing property in his virtues. I feel as warmly when he is praised, as the lover when he hears applause of his engaged maiden. We over-estimate the conscience of our friend. His goodness seems better than our goodness, his nature finer, his temptations less. Every thing that is his, his name, his form, his dress, books and instruments, fancy enhances. Our own thought sounds new and larger from his mouth.

Yet the systole and diastole of the heart are not without their analogy in the ebb and flow of love. Friendship, like the immortality of the soul, is too good to be believed. The lover, beholding his maiden, half knows that she is not verily that which he worships; and in the golden hour of friendship we are surprised with shades of suspicion and unbelief. We doubt that we bestow on our hero the virtues in which he shines, and afterwards worship the form to which we have ascribed this divine inhabitation. In strictness, the soul does not respect men as it respects itself. In strict science all persons underlie the same condition of an infinite remoteness. Shall we fear to cool our love by facing the fact, by mining for the metaphysical foundation of this Elysian† temple? Shall I not be as real as the things I see? If I am, I shall not fear to know them for what they are. Their essence is not less beautiful than their appearance, though it needs finer organs for its apprehension. The root of the plant is not unsightly to science, though for chaplets† and festoons† we cut the stem short. And I must hazard the production of the bald fact amidst these pleasing reveries, though it should prove an Egyptian skull at our banquet. A man who stands united with his thought conceives magnificently of himself. He is conscious of a universal success, even though bought by uniform particular failures. No advantages, no powers, no gold or force, can be any match for him. I cannot choose but rely on my own poverty more than on your wealth. I cannot make your consciousness tantamount to mine. Only the star dazzles; the planet has a faint, moon-like ray. I hear what you say of the admirable parts and tried temper of the party you praise, but I see well that, for all his purple cloaks I shall not like him, unless he is at last a poor Greek like me. I cannot deny it, O friend, that the vast shadow of the Phenomenal includes thee also in its pied and painted immensity,—thee also, compared with whom all else is shadow. Thou art not Being, as Truth is, as Justice is,—thou art not my soul, but a picture and effigy of that. Thou hast come to me lately, and already thou art seizing thy hat and cloak. Is it not that the soul puts forth friends as the tree puts forth leaves, and presently, by the germination of new buds, extrudes the old leaf? The law of nature is alternation for evermore. Each electrical state superinduces the opposite. The soul environs itself with friends that it may enter into a grander self-acquaintance or solitude; and it goes alone for a season, that it may exalt its conversation or society. This method betrays itself along the whole history of our personal relations. The instinct of affection revives the hope of union with our mates, and the returning sense of insulation recalls us from the chase. Thus every man passes his life in the search after friendship and if he should record his true sentiment, he might write a letter like this to each new candidate for his love:

> DEAR FRIEND, If I was sure of thee, sure of thy capacity, sure to match my mood with thine, I should never think again of trifles in relation to thy comings and goings. I am not very wise; my moods are quite attainable: and I respect thy genius: it is to me as yet unfathomed; yet dare I not presume in thee a perfect intelligence of me, and so thou art to me a delicious torment. Thine ever, or never.

Yet these uneasy pleasures and fine pains are for curiosity and not for life. They are not to be indulged. This is to weave cobweb, and not cloth. Our friendships hurry to short and poor conclusions, because we have made them a texture of wine and dreams, instead of the tough fibre of the human heart. The laws of friendship are great, austere and eternal, of one web with the laws of nature and of morals. But we have aimed at a swift and petty benefit, to suck a sudden sweetness. We snatch at the slowest fruit in the whole garden of God, which many summers and many winters must ripen. We seek our friend not sacredly, but with an adulterate passion which would appropriate him to ourselves. In vain. We are armed all over with subtle antagonisms, which, as soon as we meet, begin to play, and translate all poetry into stale prose. Almost all people descend to meet. All association must be a compromise, and, what is worst, the very flower and aroma of the flower of each of the beautiful natures disappears as they approach each other. What a perpetual disappointment is actual society, even of the virtuous and gifted! After interviews have been compassed with long foresight we must be tormented presently by baffled blows, by sudden, unseasonable apathies, by epilepsies of wit and of animal spirits, in the hey-day of friendship and thought. Our faculties do not play us true, and both parties are relieved by solitude.

I ought to be equal to every relation. It makes no difference how many friends I have and what content I can find in conversing with each, if there be one to whom I am not equal. If I have shrunk unequal from one contest, instantly the joy I find in all the rest becomes mean and cowardly. I should hate myself, if then I made my other friends my asylum.

> The valiant warrior famoused for fight,
> After a hundred victories, once foiled,
> Is from the book of honor razed quite
> And all the rest forgot for which he toiled.

Our impatience is thus sharply rebuked. Bashfulness and apathy are a tough husk in which a delicate organization is protected from premature ripening. It would be lost if it knew itself before any of the best souls were yet ripe enough to know and own it. Respect the *naturlangsamkeit*† which hardens the ruby in a million years, and works in duration in which Alps† and Andes† come and go as rainbows. The good spirit of our life has no heaven which is the price of rashness. Love, which is the essence of God, is not for levity, but for the total worth of man. Let us not have this childish luxury in our regards, but the austerest worth; let us approach our friend with an audacious trust in the truth of his heart, in the breadth, impossible to be overturned, of his foundations.

The attractions of this subject are not to be resisted, and I leave, for the time, all account of subordinate social benefit, to speak of that select and sacred relation which is a kind of absolute, and which even leaves the language of love suspicious and common, so much is this purer, and nothing is so much divine.

I do not wish to treat friendships daintily, but with roughest courage. When they are real, they are not glass threads or frost-work, but the solidest thing we know. For now, after so many ages of experience, what do we know of nature or of ourselves? Not one step has man taken toward the solution of the problem of his destiny. In one condemnation of folly stand the whole universe of men. But the sweet sincerity of joy and peace which I draw from this alliance with my brother's soul is the nut itself whereof all nature and all thought is but the husk and shell. Happy is the house that shelters a friend! It might well be built, like a festal bower or arch, to entertain him a single day. Happier, if he know the solemnity of that relation and honor its law! It is no idle bond, no holiday engagement. He who offers himself a candidate for that covenant comes up, like an Olympian, to the great games where the first-born of the world are the competitors. He proposes himself for contest where Time, Want, Danger, are in the lists, and he alone is victor who has truth enough in his constitution to preserve the delicacy of his beauty from the wear and tear of all these. The gifts of fortune may be present or absent, but all the hap in that contest depends on intrinsic nobleness and the contempt of trifles. There are two elements that go to the composition of friendship, each so sovereign that I can detect no superiority in either, no reason why either should be first named. One is Truth. A friend is a person with whom I may be sincere. Before him I may think aloud. I am arrived at last in the presence of a man so real and equal that I may drop even those undermost garments of dissimulation, courtesy, and second thought, which men never put off, and may deal with him with the simplicity and wholeness with which one chemical atom meets another. Sincerity is the luxury allowed, like diadems and authority, only to the highest rank, *that* being permitted to speak truth, as having none above it to court or conform unto. Every man alone is sincere. At the entrance of a second person, hypocrisy begins. We parry and fend the approach of our fellow man by compliments, by gossip, by amusements, by affairs. We cover up our thought from him under a hundred folds. I knew a man who under a certain religious frenzy cast off this drapery, and omitting all compliment and commonplace, spoke to the conscience of every person he encountered, and that with great insight and beauty. At first he was resisted, and all men agreed he was mad. But persisting, as indeed he could not help doing, for some time in this course, he attained to the advantage of bringing every man of his acquaintance into true relations with him. No man would think of speaking falsely with him, or of putting him off with any chat of markets or reading-rooms. But every man was constrained by so much sincerity to face him, and what love of nature, what poetry, what symbol of truth he had, he did certainly show him. But to most of us society shows not its face and eye, but its side and its back. To stand in true relations with men in a false age is worth a fit of insanity, is it not? We can seldom go erect. Almost every man we meet requires some civility, requires to be humored;—he has some fame, some talent, some whim of religion or philanthropy in his head that is not to be questioned, and which spoils all conversation with him. But a friend is a sane man who exercises not my ingenuity, but me. My friend gives me entertainment without requiring me to stoop, or to lisp, or to mask myself. A friend therefore is a sort of paradox in nature. I who alone am, I who see nothing in nature whose existence I can affirm with equal evidence to my own, behold now the semblance of my being, in all its height, variety and curiosity, reiterated in a foreign form; so that a friend may well be reckoned the masterpiece of nature.

The other element of friendship is Tenderness. We are holden to men by every sort of tie, by blood, by pride, by fear, by hope, by lucre, by lust, by hate, by admiration, by every circumstance and badge and trifle, but we can scarce believe that so much character can subsist in another as to draw us by love. Can another be so blessed and we so pure that we can offer him tenderness? When a man becomes dear to me I have touched the goal of fortune. I find very little written directly to the heart of this matter in books. And yet I have one text which I cannot choose but remember. My author says, "I offer myself faintly and bluntly to those whose I effectually am, and tender myself least to him to whom I am the most devoted." I wish that friendship should have feet, as well as eyes and eloquence. It must plant itself on the ground, before it walks over the moon. I wish it to be a little of a citizen, before it is quite a cherub. We chide the citizen because he makes love a commodity. It is an exchange of gifts, of useful loans; it is good neighborhood; it watches with the sick; it holds the pall at the funeral; and quite loses sight of the delicacies and nobility of the relation. But though we cannot find the god under this disguise of a sutler, yet on the other hand we cannot forgive the poet if he spins his thread too fine and does not substantiate his romance by the municipal virtues of justice, punctuality, fidelity and pity. I hate the prostitution of the name of friendship to signify modish and worldly alliances. I much prefer the company of ploughboys and tin-peddlers to the silken and perfumed amity which celebrates its days of encounter by a frivolous display, by rides in a curricle and dinners at the best taverns. The end of friendship is a commerce the most strict and homely that can be joined; more strict than any of which we have experience. It is for aid and comfort through all the relations and passages of life and death. It is fit for serene days and graceful gifts and country rambles, but also for rough roads and hard fare, shipwreck, poverty and persecution. It keeps company with the sallies of the wit and the trances of religion. We are to dignify to each other the daily needs and offices of man's life, and embellish it by courage, wisdom and unity. It should never fall into something usual and settled, but should be alert and inventive and add rhyme and reason to what was drudgery.

For perfect friendship may be said to require natures so rare and costly, so well tempered each and so happily adapted, and withal so circumstanced (for even in that particular, a poet says, love demands that the parties be altogether paired), that very seldom can its satisfaction be realized. It cannot subsist in its perfection, say some of those who are learned in this warm lore of the heart, betwixt more than two. I am not quite so strict in my terms, perhaps because I have never known so high a fellowship as others. I please my imagination more with a circle of godlike men and women variously related to each other and between whom subsists a lofty intelligence. But I find this law of *one to one* peremptory for conversation, which is the practice and consummation of friendship. Do not mix waters too much. The best mix as ill as good and bad. You shall have very useful and cheering discourse at several times with two several men, but let all three of you come together and you shall not have one new and hearty word. Two may talk and one may hear, but three cannot take part in a conversation of the most sincere and searching sort. In good company there is never such discourse between two, across the table, as takes place when you leave them alone. In good company the individuals at once merge their egotism into a social soul exactly coextensive with the several consciousnesses there present. No partialities of friend to friend, no fondnesses of brother to sister, of wife to husband, are there pertinent, but quite otherwise. Only he may then speak who can sail on the common thought of the party, and not poorly limited to his own. Now this convention, which good sense demands, destroys the high freedom of great conversation, which requires an absolute running of two souls into one.

No two men but being left alone with each other enter into simpler relations. Yet it is affinity that determines *which* two shall converse. Unrelated men give little joy to each other; will never suspect the latent powers of each. We talk sometimes of a great talent for conversation, as if it were a permanent property in some individuals. Conversation is an evanescent relation,—no more. A man is reputed to have thought and eloquence; he cannot, for all that, say a word to his cousin or his uncle. They accuse his silence with as much reason as they would blame the insignificance of a dial in the shade. In the sun it will mark the hour. Among those who enjoy his thought he will regain his tongue.

Friendship requires that rare mean betwixt likeness and unlikeness that piques each with the presence of power and of consent in the other party. Let me be alone to the end of the world, rather than that my friend should overstep, by a word or a look, his real sympathy. I am equally baulked by antagonism and by compliance. Let him not cease an instant to be himself. The only joy I have in his being mine, is that the *not mine* is *mine*. It turns the stomach, it blots the daylight, where I looked for a manly furtherance or at least a manly resistance, to find a mush of concession. Better be a nettle in the side of your friend than his echo. The condition which high friendship demands is ability to do without it. To be capable that high office requires great and sublime parts. There must be very two, before there can be very one. Let it be an alliance of two large, formidable natures, mutually beheld, mutually feared, before yet they recognise the deep identity which, beneath these disparities, unites them.

He only is fit for this society who is magnanimous. He must be so to know its law. He must be one who is sure that greatness and goodness are always economy. He must be one who is not swift to intermeddle with his fortunes. Let him not dare to intermeddle with this. Leave to the diamond its ages to grow, nor expect to accelerate the births of the eternal. Friendship demands a religious treatment. We must not be wilful, we must not provide. We talk of choosing our friends, but friends are self-elected. Reverence is a great part of it. Treat your friend as a spectacle. Of course if he be a man he has merits that are not yours, and that you cannot honor if you must needs hold him close to your person. Stand aside. Give those merits room. Let them mount and expand. Be not so much his friend that you can never know his peculiar energies, like fond mammas who shut up their boy in the house until he is almost grown a girl. Are you the friend of your friend's buttons, or of his thought? To a great heart he will still be a stranger in a thousand particulars, that he may come near in the holiest ground. Leave it to girls and boys to regard a friend as property, and to suck a short and all-confounding pleasure, instead of the pure nectar of God.

Let us buy our entrance to this guild by a long probation. Why should we desecrate noble and beautiful souls by intruding on them? Why insist on rash personal relations with your friend? Why go to his house, or know his mother and brother and sisters? Why be visited by him at your own? Are these things material to our covenant? Leave this touching and clawing. Let him be to me a spirit. A message, a thought, a sincerity, a glance from him, I want, but not news, nor pottage. I can get politics and chat and neighborly conveniences from cheaper companions. Should not the society of my friend be to me poetic, pure, universal and great as nature itself? Ought I to feel that our tie is profane in comparison with yonder bar of cloud that sleeps on the horizon, or that clump of waving grass that divides the brook? Let us not vilify, but raise it to that standard. That great defying eye, that scornful beauty of his mien and action, do not pique yourself on reducing, but rather fortify and enhance. Worship his superiorities. Wish him not less by a thought, but hoard and tell them all. Guard him as thy great counterpart; have a princedom to thy friend. Let him be to thee forever a sort of beautiful enemy, untamable, devoutly revered, and not a trivial conveniency to be soon outgrown and cast aside. The hues of the opal, the light of the diamond, are not to be seen if the eye is too near. To my friend I write a letter and from him I receive a letter. That seems to you a little. To me it suffices. It is a spiritual gift worthy of him to give and of me to receive. It profanes nobody. In these warm lines the heart will trust itself, as it will not to the tongue, and pour out the prophecy of a godlier existence than all the annals of heroism have yet made good.

Respect so far the holy laws of this fellowship as not to prejudice its perfect flower by your impatience for its opening. We must be our own before we can be another's. There is at least this satisfaction in crime, according to the Latin proverb; you can speak to your accomplice on even terms. *Crimen quos inquinat, aequat.*† To those whom we admire and love, at first we cannot. Yet the least defect of self-possession vitiates, in my judgment, the entire relation. There can never be deep peace between two spirits, never mutual respect, until in their dialogue each stands for the whole world.

What is so great as friendship, let us carry with what grandeur of spirit we can. Let us be silent,—so we may hear the whisper of the gods. Let us not interfere. Who set you to cast about what you should say to the select souls, or how to say anything to such? No matter how ingenious, no matter how graceful and bland. There are innumerable degrees of folly and wisdom, and for you to say aught is to be frivolous. Wait, and thy heart shall speak. Wait until the necessary and everlasting overpowers you, until day and night avail themselves of your lips. The only money of God is God. He pays never with any thing less, or any thing else. The only reward of virtue is virtue: the only way to have a friend is to be one. You shall not come nearer a man by getting into his house. If unlike, his soul only flees the faster from you, and you shall never catch a true glance of his eye. We see the noble afar off and they repel us; why should we intrude? Late,—very late,—we perceive that no arrangements, no introductions, no consuetudes or habits of society would be of any avail to establish us in such relations with them as we desire,—but solely the uprise of nature in us to the same degree it is in them: then shall we meet as water with water: and if we should not meet them then, we shall not want them, for we are already they. In the last analysis, love is only the reflection of a man's own worthiness from other men. Men have sometimes exchanged names with their friends, as if they would signify that in their friend each loved his own soul.

The higher the style we demand of friendship, of course the less easy to establish it with flesh and blood. We walk alone in the world. Friends such as we desire are dreams and fables. But a sublime hope cheers ever the faithful heart, that elsewhere, in other regions of the universal power, souls are now acting, enduring and daring, which can love us and which we can love. We may congratulate ourselves that the period of nonage, of follies, of blunders and of shame, is passed in solitude, and when we are finished men we shall grasp heroic hands in heroic hands. Only be admonished by what you already see, not to strike leagues of friendship with cheap persons, where no friendship can be. Our impatience betrays us into rash and foolish alliances which no God attends. By persisting in your path, though you forfeit the little you gain the great. You become pronounced. You demonstrate yourself, so as to put yourself out of the reach of false relations, and you draw to you the first-born of the world,—those rare pilgrims whereof only one or two wander in nature at once, and before whom the vulgar great show as spectres and shadows merely.

It is foolish to be afraid of making our ties too spiritual, as if so we could lose any genuine love. Whatever correction of our popular views we make from insight, nature will be sure to bear us out in, and though it seem to rob us of some joy, will repay us with a greater. Let us feel if we will the absolute insulation of man. We are sure that we have all in us. We go to Europe, or we pursue persons, or we read books, in the instinctive faith that these will call it out and reveal us to ourselves. Beggars all. The persons are such as we;

the Europe, an old faded garment of dead persons; the books, their ghosts. Let us drop this idolatry. Let us give over this mendicancy. Let us even bid our dearest friends farewell, and defy them, saying 'Who are you? Unhand me; I will be dependent no more.' Ah! seest thou not, O brother, that thus we part only to meet again on a higher platform, and only be more each other's because we are more our own? A friend is Janus-faced:† he looks to the past and the future. He is the child of all my foregoing hours, the prophet of those to come, and the harbinger of a greater friend. It is the property of the divine to be reproductive.

I do then with my friends as I do with my books. I would have them where I can find them, but I seldom use them. We must have society on our own terms, and admit or exclude it on the slightest cause. I cannot afford to speak much with my friend. If he is great he makes me so great that I cannot descend to converse. In the great days, presentiments hover before me, in the firmament. I ought then to dedicate myself to them. I go in that I may seize them, I go out that I may seize them. I fear only that I may lose them receding into the sky in which now they are only a patch of brighter light. Then, though I prize my friends, I cannot afford to talk with them and study their visions, lest I lose my own. It would indeed give me a certain household joy to quit this lofty seeking, this spiritual astronomy or search of stars, and come down to warm sympathies with you; but then I know well I shall mourn always the vanishing of my mighty gods. It is true, next week I shall have languid times, when I can well afford to occupy myself with foreign objects; then I shall regret the lost literature of your mind, and wish you were by my side again. But if you come, perhaps you will fill my mind only with new visions; not with yourself but with your lustres, and I shall not be able any more than now to converse with you. So I will owe to my friends this evanescent intercourse. I will receive from them not what they have but what they are. They shall give me that which properly they cannot give me, but which emanates from them. But they shall not hold me by any relations less subtle and pure. We will meet as though we met not, and part as though we parted not.

It has seemed to me lately more possible than I knew, to carry a friendship greatly, on one side, without due correspondence on the other. Why should I cumber myself with the poor fact that the receiver is not capacious? It never troubles the sun that some of his rays fall wide and vain into ungrateful space, and only a small part on the reflecting planet. Let your greatness educate the crude and cold companion. If he is unequal he will presently pass away; but thou art enlarged by thy own shining, and no longer a mate for frogs and worms, dost soar and burn with the gods of the empyrean. It is thought a disgrace to love unrequited. But the great will see that true love cannot be unrequited. True love transcends the unworthy object and dwells and broods on the eternal, and when the poor interposed mask crumbles, it is not sad, but feels rid of so much earth and feels its independency the surer. Yet these things may hardly be said without a sort of treachery to the relation. The essence of friendship is entireness, a total magnanimity and trust. It must not surmise or provide for infirmity. It treats its object as a god, that it may deify both.

Friendship
Glossary

Friendship – The essay is frequently, but not always, preceded by an untitled poem by Emerson:

A ruddy drop of manly blood
The surging sea outweighs;
The world uncertain comes and goes,
The lover rooted stays.
I fancied he was fled,
And, after many a year,
Glowed unexhausted kindliness
Like daily sunrise there.
My careful heart was free again,—
O friend, my bosom said,
Through thee alone the sky is arched,
Through thee the rose is red,
All things through thee take nobler form
And look beyond the earth,
The mill-round of our fate appears
A sun-path in thy worth.
Me too thy nobleness has taught
To master my despair;
The fountains of my hidden life
Are through thy friendship fair.

Apollo – the Greek god of the sun, poetry, light, music, and truth, and others; he was the son of Zeus and often has "Phoebus" attached to his name.

Muses – In mythology, the muses are nine sisters, daughters of Zeus, who inspire creativity in poetry, music, art, and other disciplines. They are: Clio (history), Urania (astronomy), Thalia (comedy), Melpomene (tragedy), Erato (love poetry), Polyhymnia (song), Euterpe (lyric poetry), Terpsichore (dance), and Calliope (epic poetry).

Elysian – heavenly; Elysium was the region of the Greek underworld reserved for heroes.

chaplets – a garland of leaves worn on the head

festoons – decorative drapings of leaves or flowers

naturlangsamkeit – *[German]* "the natural slowness of time"; Emerson may have coined the word.

Alps – a major European mountain range

Andes – a mountain range in South America

Crimen...aequat – *[Latin]* "Those whom crime pollutes, it makes equal."

Janus-faced – Janus, the Roman god of gates, doorways, beginnings, and endings, is usually depicted with two faces, each looking in an opposite direction.

HENRY DAVID THOREAU

HENRY DAVID THOREAU

HENRY DAVID THOREAU is best known to most Americans as a man who divorced himself from society and lived in the woods, specifically the woods of Concord, Massachusetts, near Walden Pond, which he made famous with a small book of essays.

In the book, *Walden or Life in the Woods,* Thoreau offers his views on the duties and the rights of free men, the relationship of man to nature, the significance of solitude, the ultimate purpose of each man's existence, and numerous other beliefs he holds.

Henry David Thoreau was born in Concord, Massachusetts, on July 12, 1817. During his lifetime, the United States would struggle to deal with its territorial expansion, mechanization and labor, foreign and domestic wars, and the issue of slavery. Thoreau himself was fervently against slavery; he also chose to be incarcerated, rather than pay taxes that would support the United States' war with Mexico. Thoreau spent only one night in jail, and he explains some of his reasoning in his 1849 essay, *Civil Disobedience,* which deals with defiance against unjust laws and acts by governments. His views on effective resistance to unfair government practices are contained in the essay, which remains a bible of nonviolent resistance movements. Thoreau's theories influenced the Indian civil rights leader, Mohandas Gandhi, South African former President, Nelson Mandela, as well as the African-American head of the Civil Rights Movement, Dr. Martin Luther King, Jr.

Thoreau attended Harvard from 1833 to 1837. Upon graduating, he taught school for a time, but soon resigned his position. A bit later, Thoreau met Ralph Waldo Emerson, the founder of the Transcendentalist Movement, and they became close friends. Emerson was a patron of Thoreau's, encouraging him to write and helping him publish; Thoreau even became a tutor to Emerson's children.

During a period of disagreement with Emerson, however, Thoreau set off on his adventure in the simplification of his life, to, as the famous lines put it, "live deliberately, to front only the essential facts of life, and see if I could not learn what it had to teach, and not, when I came to die, discover that I had not lived." His experiment of living alone in a cabin in the woods lasted two years and two months. In the middle of his sojourn, he went through the experience that led him to write *Civil Disobedience*. Anyone reading the book today might call its author an early proponent of libertarian philosophy, since it begins, "I heartily accept the motto—'That government is best which governs least'."

On the day Thoreau died, May 6, 1862, the United States was in the middle of the Civil War, fighting over what freedom meant and who should be free. Thoreau's writings became part of the canon of American literature which deals with the subject, and the number of minds he has influenced about personal and political duty is beyond count.

Civil Disobedience

I heartily accept the motto, "That government is best which governs least"; and I should like to see it acted up to more readily and systematically. Carried out, it finally amounts to this, which also I believe, "That government is best which governs not at all"; and when men are prepared for it, that will be the kind of government which they will have. Government is at best but an expedient; but most governments are usually, and all governments are sometimes, inexpedient. The objections which have been brought against a standing army, and they are many and weighty, and deserve to prevail, may also at last be brought against a standing government. The standing army is only an arm of the standing government. The government itself, which is only the mode which the people have chosen to execute their will, is equally liable to be abused and perverted before the people can act through it. Witness the present Mexican war,† the work of comparatively a few individuals using the standing government as their tool; for, in the outset, the people would not have consented to this measure.

This American government,—what is it but a tradition, though a recent one, endeavoring to transmit itself unimpaired to posterity, but each instant losing some of its integrity? It has not the vitality and force of a single living man; for a single man can bend it to his will. It is a sort of wooden gun to the people themselves; and, if ever they should use it in earnest as a real one against each other, it will surely split. But it is not the less necessary for this; for the people must have some complicated machinery or other, and hear its din, to satisfy that idea of government which they have. Governments show thus how successfully men can be imposed on, even impose on themselves, for their own advantage. It is excellent, we must all allow, yet this government never of itself furthered any enterprise, but by the alacrity with which it got out of its way. It does not keep the country free. It does not settle the West. It does not educate. The character inherent in the American people has done all that has been accomplished; and it would have done somewhat more, if the government had not sometimes got in its way. For government is an expedient by which men would fain succeed in letting one another alone; and, as has been said, when it is most expedient, the governed are most let alone by it. Trade and commerce, if they were not made of India rubber, would never manage to bounce over the obstacles which legislators are continually putting in their way; and, if one were to judge these men wholly by the effects of their actions, and not partly by their intentions, they would deserve to be classed and punished with those mischievous persons who put obstructions on the railroads.

But, to speak practically and as a citizen, unlike those who call themselves no-government men, I ask for, not at once no government, but at once a better government. Let every man make known what kind of government would command his respect, and that will be one step toward obtaining it.

After all, the practical reason why, when the power is once in the hands of the people, a majority are permitted, and for a long period continue, to rule, is not because they are most likely to be in the right, nor because this seems fairest to the minority, but because they are physically the strongest. But a government in which the majority rule in all cases cannot be based on justice, even as far as men understand it. Can there not be a government in which majorities do not virtually decide right and wrong, but conscience?—in which majorities decide only those questions to which the rule of expediency is applicable? Must the citizen ever for a moment, or in the least degree, resign his conscience to the legislator? Why has every man a conscience, then? I think that we should be men first, and subjects afterward. It is not desirable to cultivate a respect for the law, so much as for the right. The only obligation which I have a right to assume, is to do at any time what I think right. It is truly enough said, that a corporation has no conscience; but a corporation of conscientious men is a corporation with a conscience. Law never made men a whit more just; and, by means of their respect for it, even the well-disposed are daily made the agents of injustice. A common and natural result of an undue respect for law is, that you may see a file of soldiers, colonel, captain, corporal, privates, powder-monkeys† and all, marching in admirable order over hill and dale to the wars, against their wills, aye, against their common sense and consciences, which makes it very steep marching indeed, and produces a palpitation of the heart. They have no doubt that it is a damnable business in which they are concerned; they are all peaceably inclined. Now, what are they? Men at all? or small moveable forts and magazines, at the service of some unscrupulous man in power? Visit the

Navy Yard, and behold a marine, such a man as an American government can make, or such as it can make a man with its black arts, a mere shadow and reminiscence of humanity, a man laid out alive and standing, and already, as one may say, buried under arms with funeral accompaniments, though it may be

> Not a drum was heard, nor a funeral note,
> As his corpse to the ramparts we hurried;
> Not a soldier discharged his farewell shot
> O'er the grave where our hero we buried.†

The mass of men serve the State thus, not as men mainly, but as machines, with their bodies. They are the standing army, and the militia, jailers, constables, posse comitatus,† etc. In most cases there is no free exercise whatever of the judgment or of the moral sense; but they put themselves on a level with wood and earth and stones; and wooden men can perhaps be manufactured that will serve the purpose as well. Such command no more respect than men of straw, or a lump of dirt. They have the same sort of worth only as horses and dogs. Yet such as these even are commonly esteemed good citizens. Others, as most legislators, politicians, lawyers, ministers, and officeholders, serve the State chiefly with their heads; and, as they rarely make any moral distinctions, they are as likely to serve the devil, without intending it, as God. A very few, as heroes, patriots, martyrs, reformers in the great sense, and men, serve the State with their consciences also, and so necessarily resist it for the most part; and they are commonly treated by it as enemies. A wise man will only be useful as a man, and will not submit to be "clay," and "stop a hole to keep the wind away,"† but leave that office to his dust at least: —

> I am too high-born to be propertied,
> To be a secondary at control,
> Or useful serving-man and instrument
> To any sovereign state throughout the world.†

He who gives himself entirely to his fellowmen appears to them useless and selfish; but he who gives himself partially to them is pronounced a benefactor and philanthropist.

How does it become a man to behave toward this American government to-day? I answer that he cannot without disgrace be associated with it. I cannot for an instant recognize that political organization as my government which is the slave's government also.

All men recognize the right of revolution; that is, the right to refuse allegiance to and to resist the government, when its tyranny or its inefficiency are great and unendurable. But almost all say that such is not the case now.

But such was the case, they think, in the Revolution of '75.† If one were to tell me that this was a bad government because it taxed certain foreign commodities brought to its ports, it is most probable that I should not make an ado about it, for I can do without them: all machines have their friction; and possibly this does enough good to counterbalance the evil. At any rate, it is a great evil to make a stir about it. But when the friction comes to have its machine, and oppression and robbery are organized, I say, let us not have such a machine any longer. In other words, when a sixth of the population of a nation which has undertaken to be the refuge of liberty are slaves, and a whole country is unjustly overrun and conquered by a foreign army, and subjected to military law, I think that it is not too soon for honest men to rebel and revolutionize. What makes this duty the more urgent is the fact, that the country so overrun is not our own, but ours is the invading army.

Paley,† a common authority with many on moral questions, in his chapter on the "Duty of Submission to Civil Government," resolves all civil obligation into expediency; and he proceeds to say, "that so long as the interest of the whole society requires it, that is, so long as the established government cannot be resisted or changed without public inconveniency, it is the will of God that the established government be obeyed, and no longer."—"This principle being admitted, the justice of every particular case of resistance is reduced to a computation of the quantity of the danger and grievance on the one side, and of the probability and expense of redressing it on the other." Of this, he says, every man shall judge for himself. But Paley appears never to have contemplated those cases to which the rule of expediency does not apply, in which a people, as well as an individual, must do justice, cost what it may. If I have unjustly wrested a plank from a drowning man, I must restore it to him though I drown myself. This, according to Paley, would be inconvenient. But he that would save his life, in such a case, shall lose it. This people must cease to hold slaves, and to make war on Mexico, though it cost them their existence as a people.

In their practice, nations agree with Paley; but does any one think that Massachusetts does exactly what is right at the present crisis?

> A drab of state, a cloth-o'-silver slut,
> To have her train borne up, and her soul trail in the dirt.†

Practically speaking, the opponents to a reform in Massachusetts are not a hundred thousand politicians at the South, but a hundred thousand merchants and farmers here, who are more interested in commerce and agriculture than they are in humanity, and are not prepared to do justice to the slave and to Mexico, cost what it may. I quarrel not with far-off foes, but with those who, near at home, cooperate with, and do the bidding of those far away, and without whom the latter would be harmless. We are accustomed to say, that the mass of men are unprepared; but improvement is slow, because the few are not materially wiser or better than the many. It is not so important that many should be as good as you, as that there be some absolute goodness somewhere; for that will leaven the whole lump. There are thousands who are in opinion opposed to slavery and to the war, who yet in effect do nothing to put an end to them; who, esteeming themselves children of Washington and Franklin,† sit down with their hands in their pockets, and say that they know not what to do, and do nothing; who even postpone the question of freedom to the question of free-trade, and quietly read the prices-current along with the latest advices from Mexico, after dinner, and, it may be, fall asleep over them both. What is the price-current of an honest man and patriot to-day? They hesitate, and they regret, and sometimes they petition; but they do nothing in earnest and with effect. They will wait, well disposed, for others to remedy the evil, that they may no longer have it to regret. At most, they give only a cheap vote, and a feeble countenance and Godspeed, to the right, as it goes by them. There are nine hundred and ninety-nine patrons of virtue to one virtuous man; but it is easier to deal with the real possessor of a thing than with the temporary guardian of it.

All voting is a sort of gaming, like chequers or backgammon, with a slight moral tinge to it, a playing with right and wrong, with moral questions; and betting naturally accompanies it. The character of the voters is not staked. I cast my vote, perchance, as I think right; but I am not vitally concerned that that right should prevail. I am willing to leave it to the majority. Its obligation, therefore, never exceeds that of expediency. Even voting for the right is doing nothing for it. It is only expressing to men feebly your desire that it should prevail. A wise man will not leave the right to the mercy of chance, not wish it to prevail through the power of the majority. There is but little virtue in the action of masses of men. When the majority shall at length vote for the abolition of slavery, it will be because they are indifferent to slavery, or because there is but little slavery left to be abolished by their vote. They will then be the only slaves. Only his vote can hasten the abolition of slavery who asserts his own freedom by his vote.

I hear of a convention to be held at Baltimore, or elsewhere, for the selection of a candidate for the Presidency, made up chiefly of editors, and men who are politicians by profession; but I think, what is it to any independent, intelligent, and respectable man what decision they may come to, shall we not have the advantage of his wisdom and honesty, nevertheless? Can we not count upon some independent votes? Are there not many individuals in the country who do not attend conventions? But no: I find that the respectable man, so called, has immediately drifted from his position, and despairs of his country, when his country has more reason to despair of him. He forthwith adopts one of the candidates thus selected as the only available one, thus proving that he is himself available for any purposes of the demagogue. His vote is of no more worth than that of any unprincipled foreigner or hireling native, who may have been bought. Oh for a man who is a man, and, as my neighbor says, has a bone in his back which you cannot pass your hand through! Our statistics are at fault: the population has been returned too large. How many men are there to a square thousand miles in this country? Hardly one. Does not America offer any inducement for men to settle here? The American has dwindled into an Odd Fellow,—one who may be known by the development of his organ of gregariousness, and a manifest lack of intellect and cheerful self-reliance; whose first and chief concern, on coming into the world, is to see that the alms-houses are in good repair; and, before yet he has lawfully donned the virile garb, to collect a fund for the support of the widows and orphans that may be; who, in short, ventures to live only by the aid of the mutual insurance company, which has promised to bury him decently.

It is not a man's duty, as a matter of course, to devote himself to the eradication of any, even the most enormous wrong; he may still properly have other concerns to engage him; but it is his duty, at least, to wash his hands of it, and, if he gives it no thought longer, not to give it practically his support. If I devote myself to other pursuits and contemplations, I must first see, at least, that I do not pursue them sitting upon another man's shoulders. I must get off him first, that he may pursue his contemplations too. See what gross inconsistency is tolerated. I have heard some of my townsmen say, "I should like to have them order me out to help put down an insurrection of the slaves, or to march to Mexico,—see if I would go"; and yet these very men have each, directly by their allegiance, and so indirectly, at least, by their money, furnished a substitute. The soldier is applauded who refuses to serve in an unjust war by those who do not refuse to sustain the unjust government which makes the war; is applauded by those whose own act and authority he disregards and sets at nought; as if the State were penitent to that degree that it hired one to scourge it while it sinned, but not to that degree that it left off sinning for a moment. Thus, under the name of order and civil government, we are all made at last to pay homage to and support our own meanness. After the first blush of sin, comes its indifference; and from immoral it becomes, as it were, unmoral, and not quite unnecessary to that life which we have made.

The broadest and most prevalent error requires the most disinterested virtue to sustain it. The slight reproach to which the virtue of patriotism is commonly liable, the noble are most likely to incur. Those who, while they disapprove of the character and measures of a government, yield to it their allegiance and support, are undoubtedly its most conscientious supporters, and so frequently the most serious obstacles to reform. Some are petitioning the State to dissolve the Union,† to disregard the requisitions of the President. Why do they not dissolve it themselves,—the union between themselves and the State,—and refuse to pay their quota into its treasury? Do not they stand in the same relation to the State, that the State does to the Union? And have not the same reasons prevented the State from resisting the Union, which have prevented them from resisting the State?

How can a man be satisfied to entertain an opinion merely, and enjoy it? Is there any enjoyment in it, if his opinion is that he is aggrieved? If you are cheated out of a single dollar by your neighbor, you do not rest satisfied with knowing that you are cheated, or with saying that you are cheated, or even with petitioning him to pay you your due; but you take effectual steps at once to obtain the full amount, and see that you are never cheated again. Action from principle,—the perception and the performance of right,—changes things and relations; it is essentially revolutionary, and does not consist wholly with any thing which was. It not only divides states and churches, it divides families; aye, it divides the individual, separating the diabolical in him from the divine.

Unjust laws exist: shall we be content to obey them, or shall we endeavor to amend them, and obey them until we have succeeded, or shall we transgress them at once? Men generally, under such a government as this, think that they ought to wait until they have persuaded the majority to alter them. They think that, if they should resist, the remedy would be worse than the evil. But it is the fault of the government itself that the remedy is worse than the evil. It makes it worse. Why is it not more apt to anticipate and provide for reform? Why does it not cherish its wise minority? Why does it cry and resist before it is hurt? Why does it not encourage its citizens to be on the alert to point out its faults, and do better than it would have them? Why does it always crucify Christ, and excommunicate Copernicus and Luther,† and pronounce Washington and Franklin rebels?

One would think, that a deliberate and practical denial of its authority, was the only offence never contemplated by government; else, why has it not assigned its definite, its suitable and proportionate penalty? If a man who has no property refuses but once to earn nine shillings for the State, he is put in prison for a period unlimited by any law that I know, and determined only by the discretion of those who placed him there; but if he should steal ninety times nine shillings from the State, he is soon permitted to go at large again.

If the injustice is part of the necessary friction of the machine of government, let it go, let it go: perchance it will wear smooth,—certainly the machine will wear out. If the injustice has a spring, or a pulley, or a rope, or a crank, exclusively for itself, then perhaps you may consider whether the remedy will not be worse than the evil; but if it is of such a nature that it requires you to be the agent of injustice to another, then, I say, break the law.

Let your life be a counter friction to stop the machine. What I have to do is to see, at any rate, that I do not lend myself to the wrong which I condemn. As for adopting the ways which the State has provided for remedying the evil, I know not of such ways. They take too much time, and a man's life will be gone. I have other affairs to attend to. I came into this world, not chiefly to make this a good place to live in, but to live in it, be it good or bad. A man has not every thing to do, but something; and because he cannot do everything, it is not necessary that he should do something wrong. It is not my business to be petitioning the governor or the legislature any more than it is theirs to petition me; and, if they should not hear my petition, what should I do then? But in this case the State has provided no way: its very Constitution is the evil. This may seem to be harsh and stubborn and unconciliatory; but it is to treat with the utmost kindness and consideration the only spirit that can appreciate or deserves it. So is all change for the better, like birth and death which convulse the body.

I do not hesitate to say, that those who call themselves abolitionists should at once effectually withdraw their support, both in person and property, from the government of Massachusetts, and not wait till they constitute a majority of one, before they suffer the right to prevail through them. I think that it is enough if they have God on their side, without waiting for that other one. Moreover, any man more right than his neighbors, constitutes a majority of one already.

I meet this American government, or its representative the State government, directly, and face to face, once a year, no more, in the person of its tax-gatherer; this is the only mode in which a man situated as I am necessarily meets it; and it then says distinctly, Recognize me; and the simplest, the most effectual, and, in the present posture of affairs, the indispensablest mode of treating with it on this head, of expressing your little satisfaction with and love for it, is to deny it then. My civil neighbor, the tax-gatherer, is the very man I have to deal with,—for it is, after all, with men and not with parchment that I quarrel,—and he has voluntarily chosen to be an agent of the government. How shall he ever know well what he is and does as an officer of the government, or as a man, until he is obliged to consider whether he shall treat me, his neighbor, for whom he has respect, as a neighbor and well-disposed man, or as a maniac and disturber of the peace, and see if he can get over this obstruction to his neighborliness without a ruder and more impetuous thought or speech corresponding with his action? I know this well, that if one thousand, if one hundred, if ten men whom I could name,—if ten honest men only,—aye, if one honest man, in this State of Massachusetts, ceasing to hold slaves, were actually to withdraw from this copartnership, and be locked up in the county jail therefor, it would be the abolition of slavery in America. For it matters not how small the beginning may seem to be: what is once well done is done for ever. But we love better to talk about it: that we say is our mission. Reform keeps many scores of newspapers in its service, but not one man. If my esteemed neighbor, the State's ambassador, who will devote his days to the settlement of the question of human rights in the Council Chamber, instead of being threatened with the prisons of Carolina, were to sit down the prisoner of Massachusetts, that State which is so anxious to foist the sin of slavery upon her sister,—though at present she can discover only an act of inhospitality to be the ground of a quarrel with her,—the Legislature would not wholly waive the subject the following winter.

Under a government which imprisons any unjustly, the true place for a just man is also a prison. The proper place to-day, the only place which Massachusetts has provided for her freer and less desponding spirits, is in her prisons, to be put out and locked out of the State by her own act, as they have already put themselves out by their principles. It is there that the fugitive slave, and the Mexican prisoner on parole, and the Indian come to plead the wrongs of his race, should find them; on that separate, but more free and honorable ground, where the State places those who are not with her, against her,—the only house in a slave-state in which a free man can abide with honor. If any think that their influence would be lost there, and their voices no longer afflict the ear of the State, that they would not be as an enemy within its walls, they do not know by how much truth is stronger than error, nor how much more eloquently and effectively he can combat injustice who has experienced a little in his own person. Cast your whole vote, not a strip of paper merely, but your whole influence. A minority is powerless while it conforms to the majority; it is not even a minority then; but it is irresistible when it clogs by its whole weight. If the alternative is to keep all just men in prison, or give up war and slavery, the State will not hesitate which to choose. If a thousand men were not to pay their tax-bills this year, that would not be a violent and bloody measure, as it would be to pay them, and enable the State to commit violence and shed innocent blood. This is, in fact, the definition of a peaceable revolution if any such is possible. If the tax-gatherer, or any other public officer, asks me, as one has done, "But what shall I do?" my answer is, "If you really wish to do any thing, resign your office." When the subject has refused allegiance, and the officer has resigned his office, then the revolution is accomplished. But even suppose blood should flow. Is there not a sort of blood shed when the conscience is wounded? Through this wound a man's real manhood and immortality flow out, and he bleeds to an everlasting death. I see this blood flowing now.

I have contemplated the imprisonment of the offender, rather than the seizure of his goods,—though both will serve the same purpose,—because they who assert the purest right, and consequently are most dangerous to a corrupt State, commonly have not spent much time in accumulating property. To such the State renders comparatively small service, and a slight tax is wont to appear exorbitant, particularly if they are obliged to earn it by special labor with their hands. If there were one who lived wholly without the use of money, the State itself would hesitate to demand it of him. But the rich man—not to make any invidious comparison—is always sold to the institution which makes him rich. Absolutely speaking, the more money, the less virtue; for money comes between a man and his objects, and obtains them for him; and it was certainly no great virtue to obtain it. It puts to rest many questions which he would otherwise be taxed to answer; while the only new question which it puts is the hard but superfluous one, how to spend it. Thus his moral ground is taken from under his feet. The opportunities of living are diminished in proportion as what are called the "means" are increased. The best thing a man can do for his culture when he is rich is to endeavour to carry out those schemes which he entertained when he was poor. Christ answered the Herodians according to their condition. "Show me the tribute-money,"[†] said he;—and one took a penny out of his pocket;—If you use money which has the image of Caesar on it, and which he has made current and valuable, that is, if you are men of the State, and gladly enjoy the advantages of Caesar's government, then pay him back some of his own when he demands it; "Render therefore to Caesar that which is Caesar's, and to God those things which are God's,"[†]—leaving them no wiser than before as to which was which; for they did not wish to know.

When I converse with the freest of my neighbors, I perceive that, whatever they may say about the magnitude and seriousness of the question, and their regard for the public tranquillity, the long and the short of the matter is, that they cannot spare the protection of the existing government, and they dread the consequences of disobedience to it to their property and families. For my own part, I should not like to think that I ever rely on the protection of the State. But, if I deny the authority of the State when it presents its tax-bill, it will soon take and waste all my property, and so harass me and my children without end. This is hard. This makes it impossible for a man to live honestly and at the same time comfortably in outward respects. It will not be worth the while to accumulate progeny; that would be sure to go again. You must hire or squat somewhere, and raise but a small crop, and eat that soon. You must live within yourself, and depend upon yourself, always tucked up and ready for a start, and not have many affairs. A man may grow rich in Turkey even, if he will be in all respects a good subject of the Turkish government. Confucius[†] said,—"If a State is governed by the principles of reason, poverty and misery are subjects of shame; if a State is not governed by the principles of reason, riches and honors are the subjects of shame." No: until I want the protection of Massachusetts to be extended to me in some distant southern port, where my liberty is endangered, or until I am bent solely on building up an estate at home by peaceful enterprise, I can afford to refuse allegiance to Massachusetts, and her right to my property and life. It costs me less in every sense to incur the penalty of disobedience to the State, than it would to obey. I should feel as if I were worth less in that case.

Some years ago, the State met me in behalf of the Church, and commanded me to pay a certain sum toward the support of a clergyman whose preaching my father attended, but never I myself. "Pay it," it said, "or be locked up in the jail." I declined to pay. But, unfortunately, another man saw fit to pay it. I did not see why the schoolmaster should be taxed to support the priest, and not the priest the schoolmaster; for I was not the State's schoolmaster, but I supported myself by voluntary subscription. I did not see why the lyceum[†] should not present its tax-bill, and have the State to back its demand, as well as the church. However, at the request of the selectmen, I condescended to make some such statement as this in writing:—"Know all men by these presents, that I, Henry Thoreau, do not wish to be regarded as a member of any incorporated society which I have not joined." This I gave to the town-clerk; and he has it. The State, having thus learned that I did not wish to be regarded as a member of that church, has never made a like demand on me since; though it said that it must adhere to its original presumption that time. If I had known how to name them, I should then have signed off in detail from all the societies which I never signed on to; but I did not know where to find a complete list.

I have paid no poll-tax for six years. I was put into jail once on this account, for one night; and, as I stood considering the walls of solid stone, two or three feet thick, the door of wood and iron, a foot thick, and the iron grating which strain the light, I could not help being struck with the foolishness of that institution which treated me as if I were mere flesh and blood and bones, to be locked up. I wondered that it should have concluded at length that this was the best use it could put me and had never thought to avail itself of my services in some way. I saw that, if there was a wall of stone between me and my townsmen, there was a still more difficult one to climb or break through, before they could get to be as free as I was. I did not for a moment feel confined, and the walls seemed a great waste of stone and mortar. I felt as if I alone of all my townsmen had paid my tax. They plainly did not know how to treat me, but behaved like persons who are underbred. In every threat and in every compliment there was a blunder; for they thought that my chief desire was to stand the other side of that stone wall. I could not but smile to see how industriously they locked the door on my meditations, which followed them out again without let or hinderance, and they were really all that was dangerous. As they could not reach me, they had resolved to punish my body; just as boys, if they can not come at some person against whom they have a spite, will abuse his dog. I saw that the State was half-witted, that it was timid as a lone woman with her silver spoons, and that it did not know its friends from its foes, and I lost all my remaining respect for it, and pitied it.

Thus the State never intentionally confronts a man's sense, intellectual or moral but only his body, his senses. It is not armed with superior wit or honesty, but with superior physical strength. I was not born to be forced. I will breathe after my own fashion. Let us see who is the strongest. What force has a multitude? They only can force me who obey a higher law than I. They force me to become like themselves. I do not hear of men being forced to live this way or that by masses of men. What sort of life were that to live? When I meet a government which says to me, "Your money or your life," why should I be in haste to give it my money? It may be in a great strait, and not know what to do: I cannot help that. It must help itself; do as I do. It is not worth the while to snivel about it. I am not responsible for the successful working of the machinery of society. I am not the son of the engineer. I perceive that, when an acorn and a chestnut fall side by side, the one does not remain inert to make way for the other, but both obey their own laws, and spring and grow and flourish as best they can, till one, perchance, overshadows and destroys the other. If a plant cannot live according to its nature, it dies; and so a man.

The night in prison was novel and interesting enough. The prisoners in their shirt-sleeves were enjoying a chat and the evening air in the door-way, when I entered. But the jailer said, "Come, boys, it is time to lock up"; and so they dispersed, and I heard the sound of their steps returning into the hollow apartments. My room-mate was introduced to me by the jailer, as "a first-rate fellow and a clever man." When the door was locked, he showed me where to hang my hat, and how he managed matters there. The rooms were whitewashed once a month; and this one, at least, was the whitest, most simply furnished, and probably the neatest apartment in the town. He naturally wanted to know where I came from, and what brought me there; and, when I had told him, I asked him in my turn how he came there, presuming him to be an honest man, of course; and, as the world goes, I believe he was. "Why," said he, "they accuse me of burning a barn; but I never did it." As near as I could discover, he had probably gone to bed in a barn when drunk, and smoked his pipe there; and so a barn was burnt. He had the reputation of being a clever man, had been there some three months waiting for his trial to come on, and would have to wait as much longer; but he was quite domesticated and contented, since he got his board for nothing, and thought that he was well treated.

He occupied one window, and I the other, and I saw, that, if one stayed there long, his principal business would be to look out the window. I had soon read all the tracts that were left there, and examined where former prisoners had broken out, and where a grate had been sawed off, and heard the history of the various occupants of that room; for I found that even here there was a history and a gossip which never circulated beyond the walls of the jail. Probably this is the only house in the town where verses are composed, which are afterward printed in a circular form, but not published. I was shown quite a long list of verses which were composed by some young men who had been detected in an attempt to escape, who avenged themselves by singing them.

I pumped my fellow-prisoner as dry as I could, for fear I should never see him again; but at length he showed me which was my bed, and left me to blow out the lamp.

It was like travelling into a far country, such as I had never expected to behold, to lie there for one night. It seemed to me that I never had heard the town-clock strike before, nor the evening sounds of the village; for we slept with the windows open, which were inside the grating. It was to see my native village in the light of the middle ages, and our Concord was turned into a Rhine† stream, and visions of knights and castles passed before me. They were the voices of old burghers that I heard in the streets. I was an involuntary spectator and auditor of whatever was done and said in the kitchen of the adjacent village-inn,—a wholly new and rare experience to me. It was a closer view of my native town. I was fairly inside of it. I never had seen its institutions before. This is one of its peculiar institutions; for it is a shire town. I began to comprehend what its inhabitants were about.

In the morning, our breakfasts were put through the hole in the door, in small oblong-square tin pans, made to fit, and holding a pint of chocolate, with brown bread, and an iron spoon. When they called for the vessels again, I was green enough to return what bread I had left; but my comrade seized it, and said that I should lay that up for lunch or dinner. Soon after, he was let out to work at haying in a neighboring field, whither he went every day, and would not be back till noon; so he bade me good-day, saying that he doubted if he should see me again.

When I came out of prison,—for some one interfered, and paid the tax,—I did not perceive that great changes had taken place on the common, such as he observed who went in a youth, and emerged a tottering and gray-headed man; and yet a change had to my eyes come over the scene,—the town, and State, and country,—greater than any that mere time could effect. I saw yet more distinctly the State in which I lived. I saw to what extent the people among whom I lived could be trusted as good neighbors and friends; that their friendship was for summer weather only; that they did not greatly purpose to do right; that they were a distinct race from me by their prejudices and superstitions, as the Chinamen and Malays† are; that, in their sacrifices to humanity, they ran no risks, not even to their property; that, after all, they were not so noble but they treated the thief as he had treated them, and hoped, by a certain outward observance and a few prayers, and by walking in a particular straight though useless path from time to time, to save their souls. This may be to judge my neighbors harshly; for I believe that most of them are not aware that they have such an institution as the jail in their village.

It was formerly the custom in our village, when a poor debtor came out of jail, for his acquaintances to salute him, looking through their fingers, which were crossed to represent the grating of a jail window, "How do ye do?" My neighbors did not thus salute me, but first looked at me, and then at one another, as if I had returned from a long journey. I was put into jail as I was going to the shoemaker's to get a shoe which was mended. When I was let out the next morning, I proceeded to finish my errand, and, having put on my mended shoe, joined a huckleberry party, who were impatient to put themselves under my conduct; and in half an hour,—for the horse was soon tackled,—was in the midst of a huckleberry field, on one of our highest hills, two miles off; and then the State was nowhere to be seen.

This is the whole history of "My Prisons."

I have never declined paying the highway tax, because I am as desirous of being a good neighbor as I am of being a bad subject; and, as for supporting schools, I am doing my part to educate my fellow-countrymen now. It is for no particular item in the tax-bill that I refuse to pay it. I simply wish to refuse allegiance to the State, to withdraw and stand aloof from it effectually. I do not care to trace the course of my dollar, if I could, till it buys a man, or a musket to shoot one with,—the dollar is innocent,—but I am concerned to trace the effects of my allegiance. In fact, I quietly declare war with the State, after my fashion, though I will still make what use and get what advantage of her I can, as is usual in such cases.

If others pay the tax which is demanded of me, from a sympathy with the State, they do but what they have already done in their own case, or rather they abet injustice to a greater extent than the State requires. If they pay the tax from a mistaken interest in the individual taxed, to save his property or prevent his going to jail, it is because they have not considered wisely how far they let their private feelings interfere with the public good.

This, then, is my position at present. But one cannot be too much on his guard in such a case, lest his action be biassed by obstinacy, or an undue regard for the opinions of men. Let him see that he does only what belongs to himself and to the hour.

I think sometimes, Why, this people mean well; they are only ignorant; they would do better if they knew how: why give your neighbors this pain to treat you as they are not inclined to? But I think, again, this is no reason why I should do as they do, or permit others to suffer much greater pain of a different kind. Again, I sometimes say to myself, When many millions of men, without heat, without ill-will, without personal feeling of any kind, demand of you a few shillings only, without the possibility, such is their constitution, of retracting or altering their present demand, and without the possibility, on your side, of appeal to any other millions, why expose yourself to this overwhelming brute force? You do not resist cold and hunger, the winds and the waves, thus obstinately; you quietly submit to a thousand similar necessities. You do not put your head into the fire. But just in proportion as I regard this as not wholly a brute force, but partly a human force, and consider that I have relations to those millions as to so many millions of men, and not of mere brute or inanimate things. I see that appeal is possible, first and instantaneously, from them to the Maker of them, and, secondly, from them to themselves. But, if I put my head deliberately into the fire, there is no appeal to fire or to the Maker of fire, and I have only myself to blame. If I could convince myself that I have any right to be satisfied with men as they are, and to treat them accordingly, and not according, in some respects, to my requisitions and expectations of what they and I ought to be, then, like a good Mussulman and fatalist,† I should endeavor to be satisfied with things as they are, and say it is the will of God. And, above all, there is this difference between resisting this and a purely brute or natural force, that I can resist this with some effect; but I cannot expect, like Orpheus,† to change the nature of the rocks and trees and beasts.

I do not wish to quarrel with any man or nation, I do not wish to split hairs, to make fine distinctions, or set myself up as better than my neighbors. I seek rather, I may say, even an excuse for conforming to the laws of the land. I am but too ready to conform to them. Indeed I have reason to suspect myself on this head; and each year, as the tax-gatherer comes round, I find myself disposed to review the acts and position of the general and state governments, and the spirit of the people, to discover a pretext for conformity.

> We must affect our country as our parents,
> If at any time we alienate
> Our love or industry from doing it honor,
> We must respect effects and teach the soul
> Matter of conscience and religion,
> And not desire of rule or benefit.†

I believe that the State will soon be able to take all my work of this sort out of my hands, and then I shall be no better a patriot than my fellow-countrymen. Seen from a lower point of view, the Constitution, with all its faults, is very good; the law and the courts are very respectable; even this State and this American government are, in many respects, very admirable and rare things, to be thankful for, such as a great many have described them; but seen from a point of view a little higher, they are what I have described them; seen from a higher still, and the highest, who shall say what they are, or that they are worth looking at or thinking of at all?

However, the government does not concern me much, and I shall bestow the fewest possible thoughts on it. It is not many moments that I live under a government, even in this world. If a man is thought-free, fancy-free, imagination-free, that which is not never for a long time appearing to be to him, unwise rulers or reformers cannot fatally interrupt him.

I know that most men think differently from myself; but those whose lives are by profession devoted to the study of these or kindred subjects, content me as little as any. Statesmen and legislators, standing so completely within the institution, never distinctly and nakedly behold it. They speak of moving society, but have no resting-place without it. They may be men of a certain experience and discrimination, and have no doubt invented ingenious and even useful systems, for which we sincerely thank them; but all their wit and usefulness lie within certain not very wide limits. They are wont to forget that the world is not governed by policy and expediency. Webster[†] never goes behind government, and so cannot speak with authority about it. His words are wisdom to those legislators who contemplate no essential reform in the existing government; but for thinkers, and those who legislate for all time, he never once glances at the subject. I know of those whose serene and wise speculations on this theme would soon reveal the limits of his mind's range and hospitality. Yet, compared with the cheap professions of most reformers, and the still cheaper wisdom and eloquence of politicians in general, his are almost the only sensible and valuable words, and we thank Heaven for him. Comparatively, he is always strong, original, and, above all, practical. Still his quality is not wisdom, but prudence. The lawyer's truth is not Truth, but consistency, or a consistent expediency. Truth is always in harmony with herself, and is not concerned chiefly to reveal the justice that may consist with wrong-doing. He well deserves to be called, as he has been called, the Defender of the Constitution. There are really no blows to be given by him but defensive ones. He is not a leader, but a follower. His leaders are the men of '87.[†] "I have never made an effort," he says, "and never propose to make an effort; I have never countenanced an effort, and never mean to countenance an effort, to disturb the arrangement as originally made, by which the various States came into the Union." Still thinking of the sanction which the Constitution gives to slavery, he says, "Because it was a part of the original compact,—let it stand." Notwithstanding his special acuteness and ability, he is unable to take a fact out of its merely political relations, and behold it as it lies absolutely to be disposed of by the intellect,—what, for instance, it behooves a man to do here in America to-day with regard to slavery, but ventures, or is driven, to make some such desperate answer as the following, while professing to speak absolutely, and as a private man,—from which what new and singular code of social duties might be inferred?—"The manner," says he, "in which the government of those States where slavery exists are to regulate it, is for their own consideration, under their responsibility to their constituents, to the general laws of propriety, humanity, and justice, and to God. Associations formed elsewhere, springing from a feeling of humanity, or any other cause, have nothing whatever to do with it. They have never received any encouragement from me, and they never will."

They who know of no purer sources of truth, who have traced up its stream no higher, stand, and wisely stand, by the Bible and the Constitution, and drink at it there with reverence and humility; but they who behold where it comes trickling into this lake or that pool, gird up their loins once more, and continue their pilgrimage toward its fountain-head.

No man with a genius for legislation has appeared in America. They are rare in the history of the world. There are orators, politicians, and eloquent men, by the thousand; but the speaker has not yet opened his mouth to speak, who is capable of settling the much-vexed questions of the day. We love eloquence for its own sake, and not for any truth which it may utter, or any heroism it may inspire. Our legislators have not yet learned the comparative value of free-trade and of freedom, of union, and of rectitude, to a nation. They have no genius or talent for comparatively humble questions of taxation and finance, commerce and manufactures and agriculture. If we were left solely to the wordy wit of legislators in Congress for our guidance, uncorrected by the seasonable experience and the effectual complaints of the people, America would not long retain her rank among the nations. For eighteen hundred years, though perchance I have no right to say it, the New Testament has been written; yet where is the legislator who has wisdom and practical talent enough to avail himself of the light which it sheds on the science of legislation?

The authority of government, even such as I am willing to submit to,—for I will cheerfully obey those who know and can do better than I, and in many things even those who neither know or can do so well,—is still an impure one: to be strictly just, it must have the sanction and consent of the governed. It can have no pure right over my person and property but what I concede to it. The progress from an absolute to a limited monarchy, from a limited monarchy to a democracy, is a progress toward a true respect for the individual. Is a democracy such as we know it, the last improvement possible in government? Is it not possible to take a step further towards recognizing and organizing the rights of man? There will never be a really free and enlightened State, until the State comes to recognize the individual as a higher and independent power, from which all its own power and authority are derived, and treats him accordingly. I please myself with imagining a State at last which can afford to be just to all men, and to treat the individual with respect as a neighbor; which even would not think it inconsistent with its own repose, if a few were to live aloof from it, not meddling with it, nor embraced by it, who fulfilled all the duties of neighbors and fellow-men. A State which bore this kind of fruit, and suffered it to drop off as fast as it ripened, would prepare the way for a still more perfect and glorious State, which also I have imagined, but not yet anywhere seen.

Civil Disobedience
Glossary

Mexican war – During the war with Mexico (1846-1848) the United States fought over the territory of Texas.

powder-monkeys – [*slang*] people who set and/or carry explosives

"Not a drum…we buried." – the first stanza of Charles Wolfe's (1791-1823), poem, "The Burial of Sir John Moor at Corunna"

posse comitatus – [*Latin*] "power of the country"

"clay….the wind away" – a reference to Shakespeare's *Hamlet*: "Imperious Caesar, dead and turn'd to clay / Might stop a hole to keep the wind away" (Act V, Scene i)

"I am too…the world" – lines from Shakespeare's *King John* (Act V, Scene ii)

Revolution of '75 – a reference to the Revolutionary War (1775-1783); the Colonies rebelled against the British Empire in an attempt to establish independence from English rule. Thoreau is equating that situation to the one he is encountering in his time.

Paley – William Paley (1743-1805), was a Christian writer, utilitarian, and philosopher. The title of a chapter in his 1785 book, *Principles of Moral and Political Philosophy*, may have inspired Thoreau's essay. That chapter is called "Duty of Submission to Civil Government." He is best known for his "watchmaker analogy," which is an argument for the existence of God: The insides of a watch indicate that something intelligent constructed it, and the same argument can be made for the workings of the Universe.

"A drab of state…in the dirt." – This quotation is from Thomas Middleton's play *The Revenger's Tragedy*, first performed in 1608, in which the author depicts a decaying political situation. The word *drab* means "prostitute."

Washington and Franklin – George Washington (1732-1799), and Benjamin Franklin (1706-1790); see earlier Notes, *Franklin* and *Washington*, in the Glossary for *Self-Reliance*.

"the State to dissolve the Union" – a reference to slavery, the issue that would lead to the Civil War (1861-1865); Thoreau, however, is putting forth an argument for people not paying taxes to the treasury as a form of protest, not arguing for or against slavery here.

Copernicus and Luther – Nicolaus Copernicus (1473-1543), and Martin Luther (1483-1546); see earlier Notes, *Luther* and *Copernicus* in the Glossary for *Self-Reliance*.

"Show me the tribute-money" – Matthew 22:19 indicates that Christ says, "Show me the tax-money," but the meaning is the same: One authority, God's, is not the same as another, the State's.

"Render…which are God's" – Matthew 22:21; Thoreau is repeating Christ's words, albeit with a different thrust, to further the argument that money should be paid to the State only if the taxpayer benefits from and agrees with the policies of the State.

Confucius – Also known by many other names, including "Master Kung," Confucious (551-479), was a Chinese philosopher whose thoughts have influenced the teachings and beliefs of many cultures.

lyceum – a so-called "gymnasium," which was used both for athletics and lectures, near ancient Athens where Aristotle engaged in intellectual discourse with his students; Thoreau's point is that intellectual thought is just as important as religious thought, and one should not be taxed at the expense of the other.

Rhine – the Rhine River, one of the longest and most important rivers in Western Europe

Malays – The Malays are an ethnic group that inhabits the Malay Peninsula, south of Thailand, and parts of Sumatra and Borneo.

Mussulman and fatalist – A Mussulman refers to a someone of the Muslim faith, who, according to Thoreau, would believe that everything that happens in the world is at the direction of Allah; therefore, the beliefs indicate a type of fatalism and inevitability.

Orpheus – According to Greek mythology, Orpheus was a poet and musician and invented the lyre. Called "the father of songs," he could charm beasts and make elements of nature dance and move.

"We must…rule or benefit." – This quotation comes from George Peele's (1556-1596), play, *The Battle of Alcazar,* published in 1594.

Webster – Daniel Webster (1782-1852), was an influential statesman and leader during the pre-Civil War era. His legal counsel helped support the authority of the Federal government and set Constitutional precedents. Thoreau seems to be saying that Webster, despite his accomplishments, never questioned the government's role in an individual's life.

"the men of '87" – a reference to the framers of the Constitution

From: *Walden*

Where I Lived, And What I Lived For

At a certain season of our life we are accustomed to consider every spot as the possible site of a house. I have thus surveyed the country on every side within a dozen miles of where I live. In imagination I have bought all the farms in succession, for all were to be bought, and I knew their price. I walked over each farmer's premises, tasted his wild apples, discoursed on husbandry with him, took his farm at his price, at any price, mortgaging it to him in my mind; even put a higher price on it, took everything but a deed of it, took his word for his deed, for I dearly love to talk, cultivated it, and him too to some extent, I trust, and withdrew when I had enjoyed it long enough, leaving him to carry it on. This experience entitled me to be regarded as a sort of real-estate broker by my friends. Wherever I sat, there I might live, and the landscape radiated from me accordingly. What is a house but a *sedes*, a seat?—better if a country seat. I discovered many a site for a house not likely to be soon improved, which some might have thought too far from the village, but to my eyes the village was too far from it. Well, there I might live, I said; and there I did live, for an hour, a summer and a winter life; saw how I could let the years run off, buffet the winter through, and see the spring come in. The future inhabitants of this region, wherever they may place their houses, may be sure that they have been anticipated. An afternoon sufficed to lay out the land into orchard, wood-lot, and pasture, and to decide what fine oaks or pines should be left to stand before the door, and whence each blasted tree could be seen to the best advantage; and then I let it lie, fallow perchance, for a man is rich in proportion to the number of things which he can afford to let alone.

My imagination carried me so far that I even had the refusal of several farms, the refusal was all I wanted, but I never got my fingers burned by actual possession. The nearest that I came to actual possession was when I bought the Hollowell place, and had begun to sort my seeds, and collected materials with which to make a wheelbarrow to carry it on or off with; but before the owner gave me a deed of it, his wife—every man has such a wife—changed her mind and wished to keep it, and he offered me ten dollars to release him. Now, to speak the truth, I had but ten cents in the world, and it surpassed my arithmetic to tell, if I was that man who had ten cents, or who had a farm, or ten dollars, or all together. However, I let him keep the ten dollars and the farm too, for I had carried it far enough; or rather, to be generous, I sold him the farm for just what I gave for it, and, as he was not a rich man, made him a present of ten dollars, and still had my ten cents, and seeds, and materials for a wheelbarrow left. I found thus that I had been a rich man without any damage to my poverty. But I retained the landscape, and I have since annually carried off what it yielded without a wheelbarrow. With respect to landscapes, —

"I am monarch of all I *survey*,
My right there is none to dispute."†

I have frequently seen a poet withdraw, having enjoyed the most valuable part of a farm, while the crusty farmer supposed that he had got a few wild apples only. Why, the owner does not know it for many years when a poet has put his farm in rhyme, the most admirable kind of invisible fence, has fairly impounded it, milked it, skimmed it, and got all the cream, and left the farmer only the skimmed milk.

The real attractions of the Hollowell farm, to me, were: its complete retirement, being about two miles from the village, half a mile from the nearest neighbor, and separated from the highway by a broad field; its bounding on the river, which the owner said protected it by its fogs from frosts in the spring, though that was nothing to me; the gray color and ruinous state of the house and barn, and the dilapidated fences, which put such an interval between me and the last occupant; the hollow and lichen-covered apple trees, gnawed by rabbits, showing what kind of neighbors I should have; but above all, the recollection I had of it from my earliest voyages up the river, when the house was concealed behind a dense grove of red maples, through which I heard the house-dog bark. I was in haste to buy it, before the proprietor finished getting out some rocks, cutting down the hollow apple trees, and grubbing up some young birches which had sprung up in the pasture, or, in short, had made any more of his improvements. To enjoy these advantages I was ready to carry it on; like Atlas,† to take the world on my shoulders,—I never heard what compensation he received for that,—and do all those things which had no other motive or excuse but that I might pay for it and be unmolested in my possession of it; for I knew all the while that it would yield the most abundant crop of the kind I wanted, if I could only afford to let it alone. But it turned out as I have said.

All that I could say, then, with respect to farming on a large scale—I have always cultivated a garden—was, that I had had my seeds ready. Many think that seeds improve with age. I have no doubt that time discriminates between the good and the bad; and when at last I shall plant, I shall be less likely to be disappointed. But I would say to my fellows, once for all, As long as possible live free and uncommitted. It makes but little difference whether you are committed to a farm or the county jail.

Old Cato,† whose "De Re Rustica"† is my "Cultivator,"† says,—and the only translation I have seen makes sheer nonsense of the passage,—"When you think of getting a farm turn it thus in your mind, not to buy greedily; nor spare your pains to look at it, and do not think it enough to go round it once. The oftener you go there the more it will please you, if it is good." I think I shall not buy greedily, but go round and round it as long as I live, and be buried in it first, that it may please me the more at last.

The present was my next experiment of this kind, which I purpose to describe more at length, for convenience putting the experience of two years into one. As I have said, I do not propose to write an ode to dejection, but to brag as lustily as chanticleer in the morning, standing on his roost, if only to wake my neighbors up.

When first I took up my abode in the woods, that is, began to spend my nights as well as days there, which, by accident, was on Independence Day, or the Fourth of July, 1845, my house was not finished for winter, but was merely a defence against the rain, without plastering or chimney, the walls being of rough, weather-stained boards, with wide chinks, which made it cool at night. The upright white hewn studs and freshly planed door and window casings gave it a clean and airy look, especially in the morning, when its timbers were saturated with dew, so that I fancied that by noon some sweet gum would exude from them. To my imagination it retained throughout the day more or less of this auroral character, reminding me of a certain house on a mountain which I had visited a year before. This was an airy and unplastered cabin, fit to entertain a travelling god, and where a goddess might trail her garments. The winds which passed over my dwelling were such as sweep over the ridges of mountains, bearing the broken strains, or celestial parts only, of terrestrial music. The morning wind forever blows, the poem of creation is uninterrupted; but few are the ears that hear it. Olympus† is but the outside of the earth everywhere.

The only house I had been the owner of before, if I except a boat, was a tent, which I used occasionally when making excursions in the summer, and this is still rolled up in my garret; but the boat, after passing from hand to hand, has gone down the stream of time. With this more substantial shelter about me, I had made some progress toward settling in the world. This frame, so slightly clad, was a sort of crystallization around me, and reacted on the builder. It was suggestive somewhat as a picture in outlines. I did not need to go outdoors to take the air, for the atmosphere within had lost none of its freshness. It was not so much within-doors as behind a door where I sat, even in the rainiest weather. The Harivansa† says, "An abode without birds is like a meat without seasoning." Such was not my abode, for I found myself suddenly neighbor to the birds; not by having imprisoned one, but having caged myself near them. I was not only nearer to some of those which commonly frequent the garden and the orchard, but to those wilder and more thrilling songsters of the forest which never, or rarely, serenade a villager,—the wood thrush, the veery, the scarlet tanager, the field sparrow, the whip-poor-will, and many others.

I was seated by the shore of a small pond, about a mile and a half south of the village of Concord and somewhat higher than it, in the midst of an extensive wood between that town and Lincoln, and about two miles south of that our only field known to fame, Concord Battle Ground;† but I was so low in the woods that the opposite shore, half a mile off, like the rest, covered with wood, was my most distant horizon. For the first week, whenever I looked out on the pond it impressed me like a tarn high up on the side of a mountain, its bottom far above the surface of other lakes, and, as the sun arose, I saw it throwing off its nightly clothing of mist, and here and there, by degrees, its soft ripples or its smooth reflecting surface was revealed, while the mists, like ghosts, were stealthily withdrawing in every direction into the woods, as at the breaking up of some nocturnal conventicle. The very dew seemed to hang upon the trees later into the day than usual, as on the sides of mountains.

This small lake was of most value as a neighbor in the intervals of a gentle rain-storm in August, when, both air and water being perfectly still, but the sky over-cast, mid-afternoon had all the serenity of evening, and the wood thrush sang around, and was heard from shore to shore. A lake like this is never smoother than at such a time; and the clear portion of the air above it being, shallow and darkened by clouds, the water, full of light and reflections, becomes a lower heaven itself so much the more important. From a hill-top near by, where the wood had been recently cut off, there was a pleasing vista southward across the pond, through a wide indentation in the hills which form the shore there, where their opposite sides sloping toward each other suggested a stream flowing out in that direction through a wooded valley, but stream there was none. That way I looked between and over the near green hills to some distant and higher ones in the horizon, tinged with blue. Indeed, by standing on tiptoe I could catch a glimpse of some of the peaks of the still bluer and more distant mountain ranges in the northwest, those true-blue coins from heaven's own mint, and also of some portion of the village. But in other directions, even from this point, I could not see over or beyond the woods which surrounded me. It is well to have some water in your neighborhood, to give buoyancy to and float the earth. One value even of the smallest well is, that when you look into it you see that earth is not continent but insular. This is as important as that it keeps butter cool. When I looked across the pond from this peak toward the Sudbury meadows, which in time of flood I distinguished elevated perhaps by a mirage in their seething valley, like a coin in a basin, all the earth beyond the pond appeared like a thin crust insulated and floated even by this small sheet of interverting water, and I was reminded that this on which I dwelt was but *dry land*.

Though the view from my door was still more contracted, I did not feel crowded or confined in the least. There was pasture enough for my imagination. The low shrub oak plateau to which the opposite shore arose stretched away toward the prairies of the West and the steppes of Tartary,† affording ample room for all the roving families of men. "There are none happy in the world but beings who enjoy freely a vast horizon," —said Damodara,† when his herds required new and larger pastures.

Both place and time were changed, and I dwelt nearer to those parts of the universe and to those eras in history which had most attracted me. Where I lived was as far off as many a region viewed nightly by astronomers. We are wont to imagine rare and delectable places in some remote and more celestial corner of the system, behind the constellation of Cassiopeia's Chair,† far from noise and disturbance. I discovered that my house actually had its site in such a withdrawn, but forever new and unprofaned, part of the universe. If it were worth the while to settle in those parts near to the Pleiades† or the Hyades,† to Aldebaran† or Altair,† then I was really there, or at an equal remoteness from the life which I had left behind, dwindled and twinkling with as fine a ray to my nearest neighbor, and to be seen only in moonless nights by him. Such was that part of creation where I had squatted; —

"There was a shepherd that did live,
And held his thoughts as high
As were the mounts whereon his flocks
Did hourly feed him by."†

What should we think of the shepherd's life if his flocks always wandered to higher pastures than his thoughts?

Every morning was a cheerful invitation to make my life of equal simplicity, and I may say innocence, with Nature herself. I have been as sincere a worshipper of Aurora[†] as the Greeks. I got up early and bathed in the pond; that was a religious exercise, and one of the best things which I did. They say that characters were engraven on the bathing tub of King Tching-thang[†] to this effect: "Renew thyself completely each day; do it again, and again, and forever again." I can understand that. Morning brings back the heroic ages. I was as much affected by the faint hum of a mosquito making its invisible and unimaginable tour through my apartment at earliest dawn, when I was sitting with door and windows open, as I could be by any trumpet that ever sang of fame. It was Homer's[†] requiem; itself an Iliad and Odyssey[†] in the air, singing its own wrath and wanderings. There was something cosmical about it; a standing advertisement, till forbidden, of the everlasting vigor and fertility of the world. The morning, which is the most memorable season of the day, is the awakening hour. Then there is least somnolence in us; and for an hour, at least, some part of us awakes which slumbers all the rest of the day and night. Little is to be expected of that day, if it can be called a day, to which we are not awakened by our Genius, but by the mechanical nudgings of some servitor, are not awakened by our own newly acquired force and aspirations from within, accompanied by the undulations of celestial music, instead of factory bells, and a fragrance filling the air—to a higher life than we fell asleep from; and thus the darkness bear its fruit, and prove itself to be good, no less than the light. That man who does not believe that each day contains an earlier, more sacred, and auroral hour than he has yet profaned, has despaired of life, and is pursuing a descending and darkening way. After a partial cessation of his sensuous life, the soul of man, or its organs rather, are reinvigorated each day, and his Genius tries again what noble life it can make. All memorable events, I should say, transpire in morning time and in a morning atmosphere. The Vedas[†] say, "All intelligences awake with the morning." Poetry and art, and the fairest and most memorable of the actions of men, date from such an hour. All poets and heroes, like Memnon,[†] are the children of Aurora, and emit their music at sunrise. To him whose elastic and vigorous thought keeps pace with the sun, the day is a perpetual morning. It matters not what the clocks say or the attitudes and labors of men. Morning is when I am awake and there is a dawn in me. Moral reform is the effort to throw off sleep. Why is it that men give so poor an account of their day if they have not been slumbering? They are not such poor calculators. If they had not been overcome with drowsiness, they would have performed something. The millions are awake enough for physical labor; but only one in a million is awake enough for effective intellectual exertion, only one in a hundred millions to a poetic or divine life. To be awake is to be alive. I have never yet met a man who was quite awake. How could I have looked him in the face?

We must learn to reawaken and keep ourselves awake, not by mechanical aids, but by an infinite expectation of the dawn, which does not forsake us in our soundest sleep. I know of no more encouraging fact than the unquestionable ability of man to elevate his life by a conscious endeavor. It is something to be able to paint a particular picture, or to carve a statue, and so to make a few objects beautiful; but it is far more glorious to carve and paint the very atmosphere and medium through which we look, which morally we can do. To affect the quality of the day, that is the highest of arts. Every man is tasked to make his life, even in its details, worthy of the contemplation of his most elevated and critical hour. If we refused, or rather used up, such paltry information as we get, the oracles would distinctly inform us how this might be done.

I went to the woods because I wished to live deliberately, to front only the essential facts of life, and see if I could not learn what it had to teach, and not, when I came to die, discover that I had not lived. I did not wish to live what was not life, living is so dear; nor did I wish to practise resignation, unless it was quite necessary. I wanted to live deep and suck out all the marrow of life, to live so sturdily and Spartan-like[†] as to put to rout all that was not life, to cut a broad swath and shave close, to drive life into a corner, and reduce it to its lowest terms, and, if it proved to be mean, why then to get the whole and genuine meanness of it, and publish its meanness to the world; or if it were sublime, to know it by experience, and be able to give a true account of it in my next excursion. For most men, it appears to me, are in a strange uncertainty about it, whether it is of the devil or of God, and have *somewhat hastily* concluded that it is the chief end of man here to "glorify God and enjoy him forever."[†]

Still we live meanly, like ants; though the fable tells us that we were long ago changed into men; like pygmies we fight with cranes;[†] it is error upon error, and clout upon clout, and our best virtue has for its occasion a superfluous and evitable wretchedness. Our life is frittered away by detail. An honest man has hardly need to count more than his ten fingers, or in extreme cases he may add his ten toes, and lump the rest. Simplicity, simplicity, simplicity! I say, let your affairs be as two or three, and not a hundred or a thousand; instead of a million count half a dozen, and keep your accounts on your thumb-nail. In the midst of this chopping sea of civilized life, such are the clouds and storms and quicksands and thousand-and-one items to be allowed for, that a man has to live, if he would not founder and go to the bottom and not make his port at all, by dead reckoning,[†] and he must be a great calculator indeed who succeeds. Simplify, simplify. Instead of three meals a day, if it be necessary eat but one; instead of a hundred dishes, five; and reduce other things in proportion. Our life is like a German Confederacy,[†] made up of petty states, with its boundary forever fluctuating, so that even a German cannot tell you how it is bounded at any moment. The nation itself, with all its so-called internal improvements, which, by the way are all external and superficial, is just such an unwieldy and overgrown establishment, cluttered with furniture and tripped up by its own traps, ruined by luxury and heedless expense, by want of calculation and a worthy aim, as the million households in the land; and the only cure for it, as for them, is in a rigid economy, a stern and more than Spartan simplicity of life and elevation of purpose. It lives too fast. Men think that it is essential that the *Nation* have commerce, and export ice, and talk through a telegraph,† and ride thirty miles an hour, without a doubt, whether *they* do or not; but whether we should live like baboons or like men, is a little uncertain. If we do not get out sleepers, and forge rails, and devote days and nights to the work, but go to tinkering upon our *lives* to improve *them*, who will build railroads? And if railroads are not built, how shall we get to heaven in season? But if we stay at home and mind our business, who will want railroads? We do not ride on the railroad; it rides upon us. Did you ever think what those sleepers are that underlie the railroad? Each one is a man, an Irishman, or a Yankee man. The rails are laid on them, and they are covered with sand, and the cars run smoothly over them. They are sound sleepers, I assure you. And every few years a new lot is laid down and run over; so that, if some have the pleasure of riding on a rail, others have the misfortune to be ridden upon. And when they run over a man that is walking in his sleep, a supernumerary sleeper in the wrong position, and wake him up, they suddenly stop the cars, and make a hue and cry about it, as if this were an exception. I am glad to know that it takes a gang of men for every five miles to keep the sleepers down and level in their beds as it is, for this is a sign that they may sometime get up again.

Why should we live with such hurry and waste of life? We are determined to be starved before we are hungry. Men say that a stitch in time saves nine, and so they take a thousand stitches to-day to save nine to-morrow. As for *work*, we have n't any of any consequence. We have the Saint Vitus' dance,† and cannot possibly keep our heads still. If I should only give a few pulls at the parish bell-rope, as for a fire, that is, without setting the bell, there is hardly a man on his farm in the outskirts of Concord, notwithstanding that press of engagements which was his excuse so many times this morning, nor a boy, nor a woman, I might almost say, but would forsake all and follow that sound, not mainly to save property from the flames, but, if we will confess the truth, much more to see it burn, since burn it must, and we, be it known, did not set it on fire,—or to see it put out, and have a hand in it, if that is done as handsomely; yes, even if it were the parish church itself. Hardly a man takes a half-hour's nap after dinner, but when he wakes he holds up his head and asks, "What's the news?" as if the rest of mankind had stood his sentinels. Some give directions to be waked every half-hour, doubtless for no other purpose; and then, to pay for it, they tell what they have dreamed. After a night's sleep the news is as indispensable as the breakfast. "Pray tell me anything new that has happened to a man anywhere on this globe,"—and he reads it over his coffee and rolls, that a man has had his eyes gouged out this morning on the Wachito River; never dreaming the while that he lives in the dark unfathomed mammoth cave of this world, and has but the rudiment of an eye himself.

For my part, I could easily do without the post-office. I think that there are very few important communications made through it. To speak critically, I never received more than one or two letters in my life—I wrote this some years ago—that were worth the postage. The penny-post is, commonly, an institution through which you seriously offer a man that penny for his thoughts which is so often safely offered in jest. And I am sure that I never read any memorable news in a newspaper. If we read of one man robbed, or murdered, or killed by accident, or one house burned, or one vessel wrecked, or one steamboat blown up, or one cow run over on the Western Railroad, or one mad dog killed, or one lot of grasshoppers in the winter,—we never need read of another. One is enough. If you are acquainted with the principle, what do you care for a myriad instances and applications? To a philosopher all *news*, as it is called, is gossip, and they who edit and read it are old women over their tea. Yet not a few are greedy after this gossip. There was such a rush, as I hear, the other day at one of the offices to learn the foreign news by the last arrival, that several large squares of plate glass belonging to the establishment were broken by the pressure,—news which I seriously think a ready wit might write a twelvemonth, or twelve years, beforehand with sufficient accuracy. As for Spain, for instance, if you know how to throw in Don Carlos and the Infanta, and Don Pedro and Seville and Granada,† from time to time in the right proportions,—they may have changed the names a little since I saw the papers,—and serve up a bull-fight when other entertainments fail, it will be true to the letter, and give us as good an idea of the exact state or ruin of things in Spain as the most succinct and lucid reports under this head in the newspapers: and as for England, almost the last significant scrap of news from that quarter was the revolution of 1649; and if you have learned the history of her crops for an average year, you never need attend to that thing again, unless your speculations are of a merely pecuniary character. If one may judge who rarely looks into the newspapers, nothing new does ever happen in foreign parts, a French revolution not excepted.

What news! how much more important to know what that is which was never old! "Kieou-he-yu (great dignitary of the state of Wei) sent a man to Khoung-tseu to know his news. Khoung-tseu caused the messenger to be seated near him, and questioned him in these terms: What is your master doing? The messenger answered with respect: My master desires to diminish the number of his faults, but he cannot come to the end of them. The messenger being gone, the philosopher remarked: What a worthy messenger! What a worthy messenger!" The preacher, instead of vexing the ears of drowsy farmers on their day of rest at the end of the week,—for Sunday is the fit conclusion of an ill-spent week, and not the fresh and brave beginning of a new one,—with this one other draggle-tail of a sermon, should shout with thundering voice, "Pause! Avast! Why so seeming fast, but deadly slow?"

Shams and delusions are esteemed for soundest truths, while reality is fabulous. If men would steadily observe realities only, and not allow themselves to be deluded, life, to compare it with such things as we know, would be like a fairy tale and the Arabian Nights' Entertainments. If we respected only what is inevitable and has a right to be, music and poetry would resound along the streets. When we are unhurried and wise, we perceive that only great and worthy things have any permanent and absolute existence, that petty fears and petty pleasures are but the shadow of the reality. This is always exhilarating and sublime. By closing the eyes and slumbering, and consenting to be deceived by shows, men establish and confirm their daily life of routine and habit everywhere, which still is built on purely illusory foundations. Children, who play life, discern its true law and relations more clearly than men, who fail to live it worthily, but who think that they are wiser by experience, that is, by failure. I have read in a Hindoo book, that "there was a king's son, who, being expelled in infancy from his native city, was brought up by a forester, and, growing up to maturity in that state, imagined himself to belong to the barbarous race with which he lived. One of his father's ministers having discovered him, revealed to him what he was, and the misconception of his character was removed, and he knew himself to be a prince. So soul," continues the Hindoo philosopher, "from the circumstances in which it is placed, mistakes its own character, until the truth is revealed to it by some holy teacher, and then it knows itself to be *Brahme*."† I perceive that we inhabitants of New England live this mean life that we do because our vision does not penetrate the surface of things. We think that that *is* which *appears* to be. If a man should walk through this town and see only the reality, where, think you, would the "Mill-dam"go to? If he should give us an account of the realities he beheld there, we should not recognize the place in his description. Look at a meeting-house, or a court-house, or a jail, or a shop, or a dwelling-house, and say what that thing really is before a true gaze, and they would all go to pieces in your account of them. Men esteem truth remote, in the outskirts of the system, behind the farthest star, before Adam and after the last man. In eternity there is indeed something true and sublime. But all these times and places and occasions are now and here. God himself culminates in the present moment, and will never be more divine in the lapse of all the ages. And we are enabled to apprehend at all what is sublime and noble only by the perpetual instilling and drenching of the reality that surrounds us. The universe constantly and obediently answers to our conceptions; whether we travel fast or slow, the track is laid for us. Let us spend our lives in conceiving then. The poet or the artist never yet had so fair and noble a design but some of his posterity at least could accomplish it.

Let us spend one day as deliberately as Nature, and not be thrown off the track by every nutshell and mosquito's wing that falls on the rails. Let us rise early and fast, or break fast, gently and without perturbation; let company come and let company go, let the bells ring and the children cry,—determined to make a day of it. Why should we knock under and go with the stream? Let us not be upset and overwhelmed in that terrible rapid and whirlpool called a dinner, situated in the meridian shallows. Weather this danger and you are safe, for the rest of the way is down hill. With unrelaxed nerves, with morning vigor, sail by it, looking another way, tied to the mast like Ulysses.† If the engine whistles, let it whistle till it is hoarse for its pains. If the bell rings, why should we run? We will consider what kind of music they are like. Let us settle ourselves, and work and wedge our feet downward through the mud and slush of opinion, and prejudice, and tradition, and delusion, and appearance, that alluvion which covers the globe, through Paris and London, through New York and Boston and Concord, through Church and State, through poetry and philosophy and religion, till we come to a hard bottom and rocks in place, which we can call *reality*, and say, This is, and no mistake; and then begin, having a *point d'appui*,† below freshet and frost and fire, a place where you might found a wall or a state, or set a lamp-post safely, or perhaps a gauge, not a Nilometer,† but a Realometer, that future ages might know how deep a freshet of shams and appearances had gathered from time to time. If you stand right fronting and face to face to a fact, you will see the sun glimmer on both its surfaces, as if it were a cimeter,† and feel its sweet edge dividing you through the heart and marrow, and so you will happily conclude your mortal career. Be it life or death, we crave only reality. If we are really dying, let us hear the rattle in our throats and feel cold in the extremities; if we are alive, let us go about our business.

Time is but the stream I go a-fishing in. I drink at it; but while I drink I see the sandy bottom and detect how shallow it is. Its thin current slides away, but eternity remains. I would drink deeper; fish in the sky, whose bottom is pebbly with stars. I cannot count one. I know not the first letter of the alphabet. I have always been regretting that I was not as wise as the day I was born. The intellect is a cleaver; it discerns and rifts its way into the secret of things. I do not wish to be any more busy with my hands than is necessary. My head is hands and feet. I feel all my best faculties concentrated in it. My instinct tells me that my head is an organ for burrowing, as some creatures use their snout and fore paws, and with it I would mine and burrow my way through these hills. I think that the richest vein is somewhere hereabouts; so by the divining-rod and thin rising vapors I judge; and here I will begin to mine.

From: *Walden*

THE VILLAGE

AFTER HOEING, or perhaps reading and writing, in the forenoon, I usually bathed again in the pond, swimming across one of its coves for a stint, and washed THE DUST OF LABOR from my person, or smoothed out the last wrinkle which study had made, and for the afternoon was absolutely free. Every day or two I strolled to the village to hear some of the gossip which is incessantly going on there, circulating either from mouth to mouth, or from newspaper to newspaper, and which, taken in homeopathic doses, was really as refreshing in its way as the rustle of leaves and the peeping of frogs. As I walked in the woods to see the birds and squirrels, so I walked in the village to see the men and boys; instead of the wind among the pines I heard the carts rattle. In one direction from my house there was a colony of muskrats in the river meadows; under the grove of elms and buttonwoods in the other horizon was a village of busy men, as curious to me as if they had been prairie-dogs, each sitting at the mouth of its burrow, or running over to a neighbor's to gossip. I went there frequently to observe their habits. The village appeared to me a great news room; and on one side, to support it, as once at Redding & Company's on State Street, they kept nuts and raisins, or salt and meal and other groceries. Some have such a vast appetite for the former commodity, that is, the news, and such sound digestive organs, that they can sit forever in public avenues without stirring, and let it simmer and whisper through them like the Etesian† winds, or as if inhaling ether, it only producing numbness and insensibility to pain,—otherwise it would often be painful to hear,—without affecting the consciousness. I hardly ever failed, when I rambled through the village, to see a row of such worthies, either sitting on a ladder sunning themselves, with their bodies inclined forward and their eyes glancing along the line this way and that, from time to time, with a voluptuous expression, or else leaning against a barn with their hands in their pockets, like caryatides,† as if to prop it up. They, being commonly out of doors, heard whatever was in the wind. These are the coarsest mills, in which all gossip is first rudely digested or cracked up before it is emptied into finer and more delicate hoppers within doors. I observed that the vitals of the village were the grocery, the bar-room, the post-office, and the bank; and, as a necessary part of the machinery, they kept a bell, a big gun, and a fire-engine, at convenient places; and the houses were so arranged as to make the most of mankind, in lanes and fronting one another, so that every traveller had to run the gauntlet, and every man, woman, and child might get a lick at him. Of course, those who were stationed nearest to the head of the line, where they could most see and be seen, and have the first blow at him, paid the highest prices for their places; and the few straggling inhabitants in the outskirts, where long gaps in the line began to occur, and the traveller could get over walls or turn aside into cow-paths, and so escape, paid a very slight ground or window tax. Signs were hung out on all sides to allure him; some to catch him by the appetite, as the tavern and victualling cellar; some by the fancy, as the dry goods store and the jeweller's; and others by the hair or the feet or the skirts, as the barber, the shoemaker, or the tailor. Besides, there was a still more terrible standing invitation to call at every one of these houses, and company expected about these times. For the most part I escaped wonderfully from these dangers, either by proceeding at once boldly and without deliberation to the goal, as is recommended to those who run the gauntlet, or by keeping my thoughts on high things, like Orpheus,† who, "loudly singing the praises of the gods to his lyre, drowned the voices of the Sirens,† and kept out of danger." Sometimes I bolted suddenly, and nobody could tell my whereabouts, for I did not stand much about gracefulness, and never hesitated at a gap in a fence. I was even accustomed to make an irruption into some houses, where I was well entertained, and after learning the kernels and very last sieveful of news,—what had subsided, the prospects of war and peace, and whether the world was likely to hold together much longer,—I was let out through the rear avenues, and so escaped to the woods again.

It was very pleasant, when I stayed late in town, to launch myself into the night, especially if it was dark and tempestuous, and set sail from some bright village parlor or lecture room, with a bag of rye or Indian meal upon my shoulder, for my snug harbor in the woods, having made all tight without and withdrawn under hatches with a merry crew of thoughts, leaving only my outer man at the helm, or even tying up the helm when it was plain sailing. I had many a genial thought by the cabin fire "as I sailed." I was never cast away nor distressed in any weather, though I encountered some severe storms. It is darker in the woods, even in common nights, than most suppose. I frequently had to look up at the opening between the trees above the path in order to learn my route, and, where there was no cart-path, to feel with my feet the faint track which I had worn, or steer by the known relation of particular trees which I felt with my hands, passing between two pines for instance, not more than eighteen inches apart, in the midst of the woods, invariably, in the darkest night. Sometimes, after coming home thus late in a dark and muggy night, when my feet felt the path which my eyes could not see, dreaming and absent-minded all the way, until I was aroused by having to raise my hand to lift the latch, I have not been able to recall a single step of my walk, and I have thought that perhaps my body would find its way home if its master should forsake it, as the hand finds its way to the mouth without assistance. Several times, when a visitor chanced to stay into evening, and it proved a dark night, I was obliged to conduct him to the cart-path in the rear of the house, and then point out to him the direction he was to pursue, and in keeping which he was to be guided rather by his feet than his eyes. One very dark night I directed thus on their way two young men who had been fishing in the pond. They lived about a mile off through the woods, and were quite used to the route. A day or two after one of them told me that they wandered about the greater part of the night, close by their own premises, and did not get home till toward morning, by which time, as there had been several heavy showers in the meanwhile, and the leaves were very wet, they were drenched to their skins. I have heard of many going astray even in the village streets, when the darkness was so thick that you could cut it with a knife, as the saying is. Some who live in the outskirts, having come to town a-shopping in their wagons, have been obliged to put up for the night; and gentlemen and ladies making a call have gone half a mile out of their way, feeling the sidewalk only with their feet, and not knowing when they turned. It is a surprising and memorable, as well as valuable experience, to be lost in the woods any time. Often in a snow-storm, even by day, one will come out upon a well-known road and yet find it impossible to tell which way leads to the village. Though he knows that he has travelled it a thousand times, he cannot recognize a feature in it, but it is as strange to him as if it were a road in Siberia. By night, of course, the perplexity is infinitely greater. In our most trivial walks, we are constantly, though unconsciously, steering like pilots by certain well-known beacons and headlands, and if we go beyond our usual course we still carry in our minds the bearing of some neighboring cape; and not till we are completely lost, or turned round,—for a man needs only to be turned round once with his eyes shut in this world to be lost,—do we appreciate the vastness and strangeness of nature. Every man has to learn the points of compass again as often as be awakes, whether from sleep or any abstraction. Not till we are lost, in other words not till we have lost the world, do we begin to find ourselves, and realize where we are and the infinite extent of our relations.

One afternoon, near the end of the first summer, when I went to the village to get a shoe from the cobbler's, I was seized and put into jail, because, as I have elsewhere related,† I did not pay a tax to, or recognize the authority of, the State which buys and sells men, women, and children, like cattle, at the door of its senate-house. I had gone down to the woods for other purposes. But, wherever a man goes, men will pursue and paw him with their dirty institutions, and, if they can, constrain him to belong to their desperate odd-fellow society. It is true, I might have resisted forcibly with more or less effect, might have run "amok" against society; but I preferred that society should run "amok" against me, it being the desperate party. However, I was released the next day, obtained my mended shoe, and returned to the woods in season to get my dinner of huckleberries on Fair Haven Hill. I was never molested by any person but those who represented the State. I had no lock nor bolt but for the desk which held my papers, not even a nail to put over my latch or windows. I never fastened my door night or day, though I was to be absent several days; not even when the next fall I spent a fortnight in the woods of Maine. And yet my house was more respected than if it had been surrounded by a file of soldiers. The tired rambler could rest and warm himself by my fire, the literary amuse himself with the few books on my table, or the curious, by opening my closet door, see what was left of my dinner, and what prospect I had of a supper. Yet, though many people of every class came this way to the pond, I suffered no serious inconvenience from these sources, and I never missed anything but one small book, a volume of Homer, which perhaps was improperly gilded, and this I trust a soldier of our camp has found by this time. I am convinced, that if all men were to live as simply as I then did, thieving and robbery would be unknown. These take place only in communities where some have got more than is sufficient while others have not enough. The Pope's† Homers would soon get properly distributed.

> "Nec bella fuerunt,
> Faginus astabat dum scyphus ante dapes."

> "Nor wars did men molest,
> When only beechen bowls were in request."

"You who govern public affairs, what need have you to employ punishments? Love virtue, and the people will be virtuous. The virtues of a superior man are like the wind; the virtues of a common man are like the grass; the grass, when the wind passes over it, bends."†

From: *Walden*

THE PONDS

SOMETIMES, HAVING HAD a surfeit of human society and gossip, and worn out all my village friends, I rambled still farther westward than I habitually dwell, into yet more unfrequented parts of the town, "to fresh woods and pastures new,"† or, while the sun was setting, made my supper of huckleberries and blueberries on Fair Haven Hill, and laid up a store for several days. The fruits do not yield their true flavor to the purchaser of them, nor to him who raises them for the market. There is but one way to obtain it, yet few take that way. If you would know the flavor of huckleberries, ask the cow-boy or the partridge. It is a vulgar error to suppose that you have tasted huckleberries who never plucked them. A huckleberry never reaches Boston; they have not been known there since they grew on her three hills. The ambrosial and essential part of the fruit is lost with the bloom which is rubbed off in the market cart, and they become mere provender. As long as Eternal Justice reigns, not one innocent huckleberry can be transported thither from the country's hills.

Occasionally, after my hoeing was done for the day, I joined some impatient companion who had been fishing on the pond since morning, as silent and motionless as a duck or a floating leaf, and, after practising various kinds of philosophy, had concluded commonly, by the time I arrived, that he belonged to the ancient sect of Coenobites.† There was one older man, an excellent fisher and skilled in all kinds of woodcraft, who was pleased to look upon my house as a building erected for the convenience of fishermen; and I was equally pleased when he sat in my doorway to arrange his lines. Once in a while we sat together on the pond, he at one end of the boat, and

I at the other; but not many words passed between us, for he had grown deaf in his later years, but he occasionally hummed a psalm, which harmonized well enough with my philosophy. Our intercourse was thus altogether one of unbroken harmony, far more pleasing to remember than if it had been carried on by speech. When, as was commonly the case, I had none to commune with, I used to raise the echoes by striking with a paddle on the side of my boat, filling the surrounding woods with circling and dilating sound, stirring them up as the keeper of a menagerie his wild beasts, until I elicited a growl from every wooded vale and hillside.

In warm evenings I frequently sat in the boat playing the flute, and saw the perch, which I seem to have charmed, hovering around me, and the moon travelling over the ribbed bottom, which was strewed with the wrecks of the forest. Formerly I had come to this pond adventurously, from time to time, in dark summer nights, with a companion, and, making a fire close to the water's edge, which we thought attracted the fishes, we caught pouts with a bunch of worms strung on a thread, and when we had done, far in the night, threw the burning brands high into the air like skyrockets, which, coming down into the pond, were quenched with a loud hissing, and we were suddenly groping in total darkness. Through this, whistling a tune, we took our way to the haunts of men again. But now I had made my home by the shore.

Sometimes, after staying in a village parlor till the family had all retired, I have returned to the woods, and, partly with a view to the next day's dinner, spent the hours of midnight fishing from a boat by moonlight, serenaded by owls and foxes, and hearing, from time to time, the creaking note of some unknown bird close at hand. These experiences were very memorable and valuable to me,—anchored in forty feet of water, and twenty or thirty rods from the shore, surrounded sometimes by thousands of small perch and shiners, dimpling the surface with their tails in the moonlight, and communicating by a long flaxen line with mysterious nocturnal fishes which had their dwelling forty feet below, or sometimes dragging sixty feet of line about the pond as I drifted in the gentle night breeze, now and then feeling a slight vibration along it, indicative of some life prowling about its extremity, of dull uncertain blundering purpose there, and slow to make up its mind. At length you slowly raise, pulling hand over hand, some horned pout squeaking and squirming to the upper air. It was very queer, especially in dark nights, when your thoughts had wandered to vast and cosmogonal themes in other spheres, to feel this faint jerk, which came to interrupt your dreams and link you to Nature again. It seemed as if I might next cast my line upward into the air, as well as downward into this element, which was scarcely more dense. Thus I caught two fishes as it were with one hook.

The scenery of Walden is on a humble scale, and, though very beautiful, does not approach to grandeur, nor can it much concern one who has not long frequented it or lived by its shore; yet this pond is so remarkable for its depth and purity as to merit a particular description. It is a clear and deep green well, half a mile long and a mile and three quarters in circumference, and contains about sixty-one and a half acres; a perennial spring in the midst of pine and oak woods, without any visible inlet or outlet except by the clouds and evaporation. The surrounding hills rise abruptly from the water to the height of forty to eighty feet, though on the southeast and east they attain to about one hundred and one hundred and fifty feet respectively, within a quarter and a third of a mile. They are exclusively woodland. All our Concord waters have two colors at least; one when viewed at a distance, and another, more proper, close at hand. The first depends more on the light, and follows the sky. In clear weather, in summer, they appear blue at a little distance, especially if agitated, and at a great distance all appear alike. In stormy weather they are sometimes of a dark slate-color. The sea, however, is said to be blue one day and green another without any perceptible change in the atmosphere. I have seen our river, when, the landscape being covered with snow, both water and ice were almost as green as grass. Some consider blue "to be the color of pure water, whether liquid or solid." But, looking directly down into our waters from a boat, they are seen to be of very different colors. Walden is blue at one time and green at another, even from the same point of view. Lying between the earth and the heavens, it partakes of the color of both. Viewed from a hilltop it reflects the color of the sky; but near at hand it is of a yellowish tint next the shore where you can see the sand, then a light green, which gradually deepens to a uniform dark green in the body of the pond. In some lights, viewed even from a hilltop, it is of a vivid green next the shore. Some have referred this to the reflection of the verdure; but it is equally green there against the railroad sandbank, and in the spring, before the leaves are expanded, and it may be simply the result of the prevailing blue mixed with the yellow of the sand. Such is the color of its iris. This is that portion, also, where in the spring, the ice being warmed by the heat of the sun reflected from the bottom, and also transmitted through the earth, melts first and forms a narrow canal about the still frozen middle. Like the rest of our waters, when much agitated, in clear weather, so that the surface of the waves may reflect the sky at the right angle, or because there is more light mixed with it, it appears at a little distance of a darker blue than the sky itself; and at such a time, being on its surface, and looking with divided vision, so as to see the reflection, I have discerned a matchless and indescribable light blue, such as watered or changeable silks and sword blades suggest, more cerulean than the sky itself, alternating with the original dark green on the opposite sides of the waves, which last appeared but muddy in comparison. It is a vitreous greenish blue, as I remember it, like those patches of the winter sky seen through cloud vistas in the west before sundown. Yet a single glass of its water held up to the light is as colorless as an equal quantity of air. It is well known that a large plate of glass will have a green tint, owing, as the makers say, to its "body," but a small piece of the same will be colorless. How large a body of Walden water would be required to reflect a green tint I have never proved. The water of our river is black or a very dark brown to one looking directly down on it, and, like that of most ponds, imparts to the body of one bathing in it a yellowish tinge; but this water is of such crystalline purity that the body of the bather appears of an alabaster whiteness, still more unnatural, which, as the limbs are magnified and distorted withal, produces a monstrous effect, making fit studies for a Michael Angelo.[†]

The water is so transparent that the bottom can easily be discerned at the depth of twenty-five or thirty feet. Paddling over it, you may see, many feet beneath the surface, the schools of perch and shiners, perhaps only an inch long, yet the former easily distinguished by their transverse bars, and you think that they must be ascetic fish that find a subsistence there. Once, in the winter, many years ago, when I had been cutting holes through the ice in order to catch pickerel, as I stepped ashore I tossed my axe back on to the ice, but, as if some evil genius had directed it, it slid four or five rods directly into one of the holes, where the water was twenty-five feet deep. Out of curiosity, I lay down on the ice and looked through the hole, until I saw the axe a little on one side, standing on its head, with its helve erect and gently swaying to and fro with the pulse of the pond; and there it might have stood erect and swaying till in the course of time the handle rotted off, if I had not disturbed it. Making another hole directly over it with an ice chisel which I had, and cutting down the longest birch which I could find in the neighborhood with my knife, I made a slip-noose, which I attached to its end, and, letting it down carefully, passed it over the knob of the handle, and drew it by a line along the birch, and so pulled the axe out again.

The shore is composed of a belt of smooth rounded white stones like paving-stones, excepting one or two short sand beaches, and is so steep that in many places a single leap will carry you into water over your head; and were it not for its remarkable transparency, that would be the last to be seen of its bottom till it rose on the opposite side. Some think it is bottomless. It is nowhere muddy, and a casual observer would say that there were no weeds at all in it; and of noticeable plants, except in the little meadows recently overflowed, which do not properly belong to it, a closer scrutiny does not detect a flag nor a bulrush, nor even a lily, yellow or white, but only a few small heart-leaves and potamogetons, and perhaps a water-target or two; all which however a bather might not perceive; and these plants are clean and bright like the element they grow in. The stones extend a rod or two into the water, and then the bottom is pure sand, except in the deepest parts, where there is usually a little sediment, probably from the decay of the leaves which have been wafted on to it so many successive falls, and a bright green weed is brought up on anchors even in midwinter.

We have one other pond just like this, White Pond, in Nine Acre Corner, about two and a half miles westerly; but, though I am acquainted with most of the ponds within a dozen miles of this centre I do not know a third of this pure and well-like character. Successive nations perchance have drank at, admired, and fathomed it, and passed away, and still its water is green and pellucid as ever. Not an intermitting spring! Perhaps on that spring morning when Adam and Eve were driven out of Eden Walden Pond was already in existence, and even then breaking up in a gentle spring rain accompanied with mist and a southerly wind, and covered with myriads of ducks and geese, which had not heard of the fall, when still such pure lakes sufficed them. Even then it had commenced to rise and fall, and had clarified its waters and colored them of the hue they now wear, and obtained a patent of Heaven to be the only Walden Pond in the world and distiller of celestial dews. Who knows in how many unremembered nations' literatures this has been the Castalian Fountain?† or what nymphs presided over it in the Golden Age? It is a gem of the first water which Concord wears in her coronet.

Yet perchance the first who came to this well have left some trace of their footsteps. I have been surprised to detect encircling the pond, even where a thick wood has just been cut down on the shore, a narrow shelf-like path in the steep hillside, alternately rising and falling, approaching and receding from the water's edge, as old probably as the race of man here, worn by the feet of aboriginal hunters, and still from time to time unwittingly trodden by the present occupants of the land. This is particularly distinct to one standing on the middle of the pond in winter, just after a light snow has fallen, appearing as a clear undulating white line, unobscured by weeds and twigs, and very obvious a quarter of a mile off in many places where in summer it is hardly distinguishable close at hand. The snow reprints it, as it were, in clear white type alto-relievo.† The ornamented grounds of villas which will one day be built here may still preserve some trace of this.

The pond rises and falls, but whether regularly or not, and within what period, nobody knows, though, as usual, many pretend to know. It is commonly higher in the winter and lower in the summer, though not corresponding to the general wet and dryness. I can remember when it was a foot or two lower, and also when it was at least five feet higher, than when I lived by it. There is a narrow sand-bar running into it, with very deep water on one side, on which I helped boil a kettle of chowder, some six rods from the main shore, about the year 1824, which it has not been possible to do for twenty-five years; and, on the other hand, my friends used to listen with incredulity when I told them, that a few years later I was accustomed to fish from a boat in a secluded cove in the woods, fifteen rods from the only shore they knew, which place was long since converted into a meadow. But the pond has risen steadily for two years, and now, in the summer of '52, is just five feet higher than when I lived there, or as high as it was thirty years ago, and fishing goes on again in the meadow. This makes a difference of level, at the outside, of six or seven feet; and yet the water shed by the surrounding hills is insignificant in amount, and this overflow must be referred to causes which affect the deep springs. This same summer the pond has begun to fall again. It is remarkable that this fluctuation, whether periodical or not, appears thus to require many years for its accomplishment. I have observed one rise and a part of two falls, and I expect that a dozen or fifteen years hence the water will again be as low as I have ever known it. Flint's Pond, a mile eastward, allowing for the disturbance occasioned by its inlets and outlets, and the smaller intermediate ponds also, sympathize with Walden, and recently attained their greatest height at the same time with the latter. The same is true, as far as my observation goes, of White Pond.

This rise and fall of Walden at long intervals serves this use at least; the water standing at this great height for a year or more, though it makes it difficult to walk round it, kills the shrubs and trees which have sprung up about its edge since the last rise,—pitch pines, birches, alders, aspens, and others,—and, falling again, leaves an unobstructed shore; for, unlike many ponds and all waters which are subject to a daily tide, its shore is cleanest when the water is lowest. On the side of the pond next my house a row of pitch pines, fifteen feet high, has been killed and tipped over as if by a lever, and thus a stop put to their encroachments; and their size indicates how many years have elapsed since the last rise to this height. By this fluctuation the pond asserts its title to a shore, and thus the *shore* is *shorn*, and the trees cannot hold it by right of possession. These are the lips of the lake, on which no beard grows. It licks its chaps from time to time. When the water is at its height, the alders, willows, and maples send forth a mass of fibrous red roots several feet long from all sides of their stems in the water, and to the height of three or four feet from the ground, in the effort to maintain themselves; and I have known the high blue-berry bushes about the shore, which commonly produce no fruit, bear an abundant crop under these circumstances.

Some have been puzzled to tell how the shore became so regularly paved. My townsmen have all heard the tradition—the oldest people tell me that they heard it in their youth—that anciently the Indians were holding a pow-wow upon a hill here, which rose as high into the heavens as the pond now sinks deep into the earth, and they used much profanity, as the story goes, though this vice is one of which the Indians were never guilty, and while they were thus engaged the hill shook and suddenly sank, and only one old squaw, named Walden, escaped, and from her the pond was named. It has been conjectured that when the hill shook these stones rolled down its side and became the present shore. It is very certain, at any rate, that once there was no pond here, and now there is one; and this Indian fable does not in any respect conflict with the account of that ancient settler whom I have mentioned, who remembers so well when he first came here with his divining-rod, saw a thin vapor rising from the sward, and the hazel pointed steadily downward, and he concluded to dig a well here. As for the stones, many still think that they are hardly to be accounted for by the action of the waves on these hills; but I observe that the surrounding hills are remarkably full of the same kind of stones, so that they have been obliged to pile them up in walls on both sides of the railroad cut nearest the pond; and, moreover, there are most stones where the shore is most abrupt; so that, unfortunately, it is no longer a mystery to me. I detect the paver. If the name was not derived from that of some English locality,—Saffron Walden, for instance,—one might suppose that it was called originally *Walled-in* Pond.

The pond was my well ready dug. For four months in the year its water is as cold as it is pure at all times; and I think that it is then as good as any, if not the best, in the town. In the winter, all water which is exposed to the air is colder than springs and wells which are protected from it. The temperature of the pond water which had stood in the room where I sat from five o'clock in the afternoon till noon the next day, the sixth of March, 1846, the thermometer having been up to 65° or 70° some of the time, owing partly to the sun on the roof, was 42°, or one degree colder than the water of one of the coldest wells in the village just drawn. The temperature of the Boiling Spring the same day was 45°, or the warmest of any water tried, though it is the coldest that I know of in summer, when, beside, shallow and stagnant surface water is not mingled with it. Moreover, in summer, Walden never becomes so warm as most water which is exposed to the sun, on account of its depth. In the warmest weather I usually placed a pailful in my cellar, where it became cool in the night, and remained so during the day; though I also resorted to a spring in the neighborhood. It was as good when a week old as the day it was dipped, and had no taste of the pump. Whoever camps for a week in summer by the shore of a pond, needs only bury a pail of water a few feet deep in the shade of his camp to be independent of the luxury of ice.

There have been caught in Walden pickerel, one weighing seven pounds,—to say nothing of another which carried off a reel with great velocity, which the fisherman safely set down at eight pounds because he did not see him,—perch and pouts, some of each weighing over two pounds, shiners, chivins or roach (*Leuciscus pulchellus*), a very few breams, and a couple of eels, one weighing four pounds,—I am thus particular because the weight of a fish is commonly its only title to fame, and these are the only eels I have heard of here;—also, I have a faint recollection of a little fish some five inches long, with silvery sides and a greenish back, somewhat dace-like in its character, which I mention here chiefly to link my facts to fable. Nevertheless, this pond is not very fertile in fish. Its pickerel, though not abundant, are its chief boast. I have seen at one time lying on the ice pickerel of at least three different kinds: a long and shallow one, steel-colored, most like those caught in the river; a bright golden kind, with greenish reflections and remarkably deep, which is the most common here; and another, golden-colored, and shaped like the last, but peppered on the sides with small dark brown or black spots, intermixed with a few faint blood-red ones, very much like a trout. The specific name *reticulatus* would not apply to this; it should be *guttatus* rather. These are all very firm fish, and weigh more than their size promises. The shiners, pouts, and perch also, and indeed all the fishes which inhabit this pond, are much cleaner, handsomer, and firmer-fleshed than those in the river and most other ponds, as the water is purer, and they can easily be distinguished from them. Probably many ichthyologists would make new varieties of some of them. There are also a clean race of frogs and tortoises, and a few mussels in it; muskrats and minks leave their traces about it, and occasionally a travelling mud-turtle visits it. Sometimes, when I pushed off my boat in the morning, I disturbed a great mud-turtle which had secreted himself under the boat in the night. Ducks and geese frequent it in the spring and fall, the white-bellied swallows (*Hirundo bicolor*) skim over it, and the peetweets (*Totanus macularius*) "teeter" along its stony shores all summer. I have sometimes disturbed a fish hawk sitting on a white pine over the water; but I doubt if it is ever profaned by the wind of a gull, like Fair Haven. At most, it tolerates one annual loon. These are all the animals of consequence which frequent it now.

You may see from a boat, in calm weather, near the sandy eastern shore, where the water is eight or ten feet deep, and also in some other parts of the pond, some circular heaps half a dozen feet in diameter by a foot in height, consisting of small stones less than a hen's egg in size, where all around is bare sand. At first you wonder if the Indians could have formed them on the ice for any purpose, and so, when the ice melted, they sank to the bottom; but they are too regular and some of them plainly too fresh for that. They are similar to those found in rivers; but as there are no suckers nor lampreys here, I know not by what fish they could be made. Perhaps they are the nests of the chivin. These lend a pleasing mystery to the bottom.

The shore is irregular enough not to be monotonous. I have in my mind's eye the western, indented with deep bays, the bolder northern, and the beautifully scalloped southern shore, where successive capes overlap each other and suggest unexplored coves between. The forest has never so good a setting, nor is so distinctly beautiful, as when seen from the middle of a small lake amid hills which rise from the water's edge; for the water in which it is reflected not only makes the best foreground in such a case, but, with its winding shore, the most natural and agreeable boundary to it. There is no rawness nor imperfection in its edge there, as where the axe has cleared a part, or a cultivated field abuts on it. The trees have ample room to expand on the water side, and each sends forth its most vigorous branch in that direction. There Nature has woven a natural selvage, and the eye rises by just gradations from the low shrubs of the shore to the highest trees. There are few traces of man's hand to be seen. The water laves the shore as it did a thousand years ago.

A lake is the landscape's most beautiful and expressive feature. It is earth's eye; looking into which the beholder measures the depth of his own nature. The fluviatile trees next the shore are the slender eyelashes which fringe it, and the wooded hills and cliffs around are its overhanging brows.

Standing on the smooth sandy beach at the east end of the pond, in a calm September afternoon, when a slight haze makes the opposite shore-line indistinct, I have seen whence came the expression, "the glassy surface of a lake." When you invert your head, it looks like a thread of finest gossamer stretched across the valley, and gleaming against the distant pine woods, separating one stratum of the atmosphere from another. You would think that you could walk dry under it to the opposite hills, and that the swallows which skim over might perch on it. Indeed, they sometimes dive below this line, as it were by mistake, and are undeceived. As you look over the pond westward you are obliged to employ both your hands to defend your eyes against the reflected as well as the true sun, for they are equally bright; and if, between the two, you survey its surface critically, it is literally as smooth as glass, except where the skater insects, at equal intervals scattered over its whole extent, by their motions in the sun produce the finest imaginable sparkle on it, or, perchance, a duck plumes itself, or, as I have said, a swallow skims so low as to touch it. It may be that in the distance a fish describes an arc of three or four feet in the air, and there is one bright flash where it emerges, and another where it strikes the water; sometimes the whole silvery arc is revealed; or here and there, perhaps, is a thistle-down floating on its surface, which the fishes dart at and so dimple it again. It is like molten glass cooled but not congealed, and the few motes in it are pure and beautiful like the imperfections in glass. You may often detect a yet smoother and darker water, separated from the rest as if by an invisible cobweb, boom of the water nymphs, resting on it. From a hilltop you can see a fish leap in almost any part; for not a pickerel or shiner picks an insect from this smooth surface but it manifestly disturbs the equilibrium of the whole lake. It is wonderful with what elaborateness this simple fact is advertised,—this piscine murder will out,—and from my distant perch I distinguish the circling undulations when they are half a dozen rods in diameter. You can even detect a water-bug (*Gyrinus*) ceaselessly progressing over the smooth surface a quarter of a mile off; for they furrow the water slightly, making a conspicuous ripple bounded by two diverging lines, but the skaters glide over it without rippling it perceptibly. When the surface is considerably agitated there are no skaters nor water-bugs on it, but apparently, in calm days, they leave their havens and adventurously glide forth from the shore by short impulses till they completely cover it. It is a soothing employment, on one of those fine days in the fall when all the warmth of the sun is fully appreciated, to sit on a stump on such a height as this, overlooking the pond, and study the dimpling circles which are incessantly inscribed on its otherwise invisible surface amid the reflected skies and trees. Over this great expanse there is no disturbance but it is thus at once gently smoothed away and assuaged, as, when a vase of water is jarred, the trembling circles seek the shore and all is smooth again. Not a fish can leap or an insect fall on the pond but it is thus reported in circling dimples, in lines of beauty, as it were the constant welling up of its fountain, the gentle pulsing of its life, the heaving of its breast. The thrills of joy and thrills of pain are undistinguishable. How peaceful the phenomena of the lake! Again the works of man shine as in the spring. Ay, every leaf and twig and stone and cobweb sparkles now at mid-afternoon as when covered with dew in a spring morning. Every motion of an oar or an insect produces a flash of light; and if an oar falls, how sweet the echo!

In such a day, in September or October, Walden is a perfect forest mirror, set round with stones as precious to my eye as if fewer or rarer. Nothing so fair, so pure, and at the same time so large, as a lake, perchance, lies on the surface of the earth. Sky water. It needs no fence. Nations come and go without defiling it. It is a mirror which no stone can crack, whose quicksilver will never wear off, whose gilding Nature continually repairs; no storms, no dust, can dim its surface ever fresh;—a mirror in which all impurity presented to it sinks, swept and dusted by the sun's hazy brush,—this the light dust-cloth,—which retains no breath that is breathed on it, but sends its own to float as clouds high above its surface, and be reflected in its bosom still.

A field of water betrays the spirit that is in the air. It is continually receiving new life and motion from above. It is intermediate in its nature between land and sky. On land only the grass and trees wave, but the water itself is rippled by the wind. I see where the breeze dashes across it by the streaks or flakes of light. It is remarkable that we can look down on its surface. We shall, perhaps, look down thus on the surface of air at length, and mark where a still subtler spirit sweeps over it.

The skaters and water-bugs finally disappear in the latter part of October, when the severe frosts have come; and then and in November, usually, in a calm day, there is absolutely nothing to ripple the surface. One November afternoon, in the calm at the end of a rain-storm of several days' duration, when the sky was still completely overcast and the air was full of mist, I observed that the pond was remarkably smooth, so that it was difficult to distinguish its surface; though it no longer reflected the bright tints of October, but the sombre November colors of the surrounding hills. Though I passed over it as gently as possible, the slight undulations produced by my boat extended almost as far as I could see, and gave a ribbed appearance to the reflections. But, as I was looking over the surface, I saw here and there at a distance a faint glimmer, as if some skater insects which had escaped the frosts might be collected there, or, perchance, the surface, being so smooth, betrayed where a spring welled up from the bottom. Paddling gently to one of these places, I was surprised to find myself surrounded by myriads of small perch, about five inches long, of a rich bronze color in the green water, sporting there, and constantly rising to the surface and dimpling it, sometimes leaving bubbles on it. In such transparent and seemingly bottomless water, reflecting the clouds, I seemed to be floating through the air as in a balloon, and their swimming impressed me as a kind of flight or hovering, as if they were a compact flock of birds passing just beneath my level on the right or left, their fins, like sails, set all around them. There were many such schools in the pond, apparently improving the short season before winter would draw an icy shutter over their broad sky-light, sometimes giving to the surface an appearance as if a slight breeze struck it, or a few rain-drops fell there. When I approached carelessly and alarmed them, they made a sudden plash and rippling with their tails, as if one had struck the water with a brushy bough, and instantly took refuge in the depths. At length the wind rose, the mist increased, and the waves began to run, and the perch leaped much higher than before, half out of water, a hundred black points, three inches long, at once above the surface. Even as late as the fifth of December, one year, I saw some dimples on the surface, and thinking it was going to rain hard immediately, the air being full of mist, I made haste to take my place at the oars and row homeward; already the rain seemed rapidly increasing, though I felt none on my cheek, and I anticipated a thorough soaking. But suddenly the dimples ceased, for they were produced by the perch, which the noise of my oars had scared into the depths, and I saw their schools dimly disappearing; so I spent a dry afternoon after all.

An old man who used to frequent this pond nearly sixty years ago, when it was dark with surrounding forests, tells me that in those days he sometimes saw it all alive with ducks and other water-fowl, and that there were many eagles about it. He came here a-fishing, and used an old log canoe which he found on the shore. It was made of two white pine logs dug out and pinned together, and was cut off square at the ends. It was very clumsy, but lasted a great many years before it became water-logged and perhaps sank to the bottom. He did not know whose it was; it belonged to the pond. He used to make a cable for his anchor of strips of hickory bark tied together. An old man, a potter, who lived by the pond before the Revolution,† told him once that there was an iron chest at the bottom, and that he had seen it. Sometimes it would come floating up to the shore; but when you went toward it, it would go back into deep water and disappear. I was pleased to hear of the old log canoe, which took the place of an Indian one of the same material but more graceful construction, which perchance had first been a tree on the bank, and then, as it were, fell into the water, to float there for a generation, the most proper vessel for the lake. I remember that when I first looked into these depths there were many large trunks to be seen indistinctly lying on the bottom, which had either been blown over formerly, or left on the ice at the last cutting, when wood was cheaper; but now they have mostly disappeared.

When I first paddled a boat on Walden, it was completely surrounded by thick and lofty pine and oak woods, and in some of its coves grape-vines had run over the trees next the water and formed bowers under which a boat could pass. The hills which form its shores are so steep, and the woods on them were then so high, that, as you looked down from the west end, it had the appearance of an amphitheatre for some kind of sylvan spectacle. I have spent many an hour, when I was younger, floating over its surface as the zephyr willed, having paddled my boat to the middle, and lying on my back across the seats, in a summer forenoon, dreaming awake, until I was aroused by the boat touching the sand, and I arose to see what shore my fates had impelled me to; days when idleness was the most attractive and productive industry. Many a forenoon have I stolen away, preferring to spend thus the most valued part of the day; for I was rich, if not in money, in sunny hours and summer days, and spent them lavishly; nor do I regret that I did not waste more of them in the workshop or the teacher's desk. But since I left those shores the woodchoppers have still further laid them waste, and now for many a year there will be no more rambling through the aisles of the wood, with occasional vistas through which you see the water. My Muse† may be excused if she is silent henceforth. How can you expect the birds to sing when their groves are cut down?

Now the trunks of trees on the bottom, and the old log canoe, and the dark surrounding woods, are gone, and the villagers, who scarcely know where it lies, instead of going to the pond to bathe or drink, are thinking to bring its water, which should be as sacred as the Ganges† at least, to the village in a pipe, to wash their dishes with!—to earn their Walden by the turning of a cock or drawing of a plug! That devilish Iron Horse, whose ear-rending neigh is heard throughout the town, has muddied the Boiling Spring with his foot, and he it is that has browsed off all the woods on Walden shore, that Trojan horse, with a thousand men in his belly, introduced by mercenary Greeks! Where is the country's champion, the Moore of Moore Hill, to meet him at the Deep Cut and thrust an avenging lance between the ribs of the bloated pest?

Nevertheless, of all the characters I have known, perhaps Walden wears best, and best preserves its purity. Many men have been likened to it, but few deserve that honor. Though the woodchoppers have laid bare first this shore and then that, and the Irish have built their sties by it, and the railroad has infringed on its border, and the ice-men have skimmed it once, it is itself unchanged, the same water which my youthful eyes fell on; all the change is in me. It has not acquired one permanent wrinkle after all its ripples. It is perennially young, and I may stand and see a swallow dip apparently to pick an insect from its surface as of yore. It struck me again to-night, as if I had not seen it almost daily for more than twenty years—Why, here is Walden, the same woodland lake that I discovered so many years ago; where a forest was cut down last winter another is springing up by its shore as lustily as ever; the same thought is welling up to its surface that was then; it is the same liquid joy and happiness to itself and its Maker, ay, and it *may* be to me. It is the work of a brave man surely, in whom there was no guile! He rounded this water with his hand, deepened and clarified it in his thought, and in his will bequeathed it to Concord. I see by its face that it is visited by the same reflection; and I can almost say, Walden, is it you?

It is no dream of mine,
To ornament a line;
I cannot come nearer to God and Heaven
Than I live to Walden even.
I am its stony shore,
And the breeze that passes o'er;
In the hollow of my hand
Are its water and its sand,
And its deepest resort
Lies high in my thought.

The cars never pause to look at it; yet I fancy that the engineers and firemen and brakemen, and those passengers who have a season ticket and see it often, are better men for the sight. The engineer does not forget at night, or his nature does not, that he has beheld this vision of serenity and purity once at least during the day. Though seen but once, it helps to wash out State Street[†] and the engine's soot. One[†] proposes that it be called "God's Drop."

I have said that Walden has no visible inlet nor outlet, but it is on the one hand distantly and indirectly related to Flint's Pond, which is more elevated, by a chain of small ponds coming from that quarter, and on the other directly and manifestly to Concord River, which is lower, by a similar chain of ponds through which in some other geological period it may have flowed, and by a little digging, which God forbid, it can be made to flow thither again. If by living thus reserved and austere, like a hermit in the woods, so long, it has acquired such wonderful purity, who would not regret that the comparatively impure waters of Flint's Pond should be mingled with it, or itself should ever go to waste its sweetness in the ocean wave?

Flint's, or Sandy Pond, in Lincoln, our greatest lake and inland sea, lies about a mile east of Walden. It is much larger, being said to contain one hundred and ninety-seven acres, and is more fertile in fish; but it is comparatively shallow, and not remarkably pure. A walk through the woods thither was often my recreation. It was worth the while, if only to feel the wind blow on your cheek freely, and see the waves run, and remember the life of mariners. I went a-chestnutting there in the fall, on windy days, when the nuts were dropping into the water and were washed to my feet; and one day, as I crept along its sedgy shore, the fresh spray blowing in my face, I came upon the mouldering wreck of a boat, the sides gone, and hardly more than the impression of its flat bottom left amid the rushes; yet its model was sharply defined, as if it were a large decayed pad, with its veins. It was as impressive a wreck as one could imagine on the seashore, and had as good a moral. It is by this time mere vegetable mould and undistinguishable pond shore, through which rushes and flags have pushed up. I used to admire the ripple marks on the sandy bottom, at the north end of this pond, made firm and hard to the feet of the wader by the pressure of the water, and the rushes which grew in Indian file, in waving lines, corresponding to these marks, rank behind rank, as if the waves had planted them. There also I have found, in considerable quantities, curious balls, composed apparently of fine grass or roots, of pipewort perhaps, from half an inch to four inches in diameter, and perfectly spherical. These wash back and forth in shallow water on a sandy bottom, and are sometimes cast on the shore. They are either solid grass, or have a little sand in the middle. At first you would say that they were formed by the action of the waves, like a pebble; yet the smallest are made of equally coarse materials, half an inch long, and they are produced only at one season of the year. Moreover, the waves, I suspect, do not so much construct as wear down a material which has already acquired consistency. They preserve their form when dry for an indefinite period.

Flint's Pond! Such is the poverty of our nomenclature. What right had the unclean and stupid farmer, whose farm abutted on this sky water, whose shores he has ruthlessly laid bare, to give his name to it? Some skin-flint, who loved better the reflecting surface of a dollar, or a bright cent, in which he could see his own brazen face; who regarded even the wild ducks which settled in it as trespassers; his fingers grown into crooked and bony talons from the long habit of grasping harpy-like;—so it is not named for me. I go not there to see him nor to hear of him; who never *saw* it, who never bathed in it, who never loved it, who never protected it, who never spoke a good word for it, nor thanked God that He had made it. Rather let it be named from the fishes that swim in it, the wild fowl or quadrupeds which frequent it, the wild flowers which grow by its shores, or some wild man or child the thread of whose history is interwoven with its own; not from him who could show no title to it but the deed which a like-minded neighbor or legislature gave him—him who thought only of its money value; whose presence perchance cursed all the shores; who exhausted the land around it, and would fain have exhausted the waters within it; who regretted only that it was not English hay or cranberry meadow,—there was nothing to redeem it, forsooth, in his eyes,—and would have drained and sold it for the mud at its bottom. It did not turn his mill, and it was no *privilege* to him to behold it. I respect not his labors, his farm where everything has its price, who would carry the landscape, who would carry his God, to market, if he could get anything for him; who goes to market *for* his god as it is; on whose farm nothing grows free, whose fields bear no crops, whose meadows no flowers, whose trees no fruits, but dollars; who loves not the beauty of his fruits, whose fruits are not ripe for him till they are turned to dollars. Give me the poverty that enjoys true wealth. Farmers are respectable and interesting to me in proportion as they are poor,—poor farmers. A model farm! where the house stands like a fungus in a muckheap, chambers for men, horses, oxen, and swine, cleansed and uncleansed, all contiguous to one another! Stocked with men! A great grease-spot, redolent of manures and buttermilk! Under a high state of cultivation, being manured with the hearts and brains of men! As if you were to raise your potatoes in the churchyard! Such is a model farm.

No, no; if the fairest features of the landscape are to be named after men, let them be the noblest and worthiest men alone. Let our lakes receive as true names at least as the Icarian Sea,† where "still the shore" a "brave attempt resounds."†

Goose Pond, of small extent, is on my way to Flint's; Fair Haven, an expansion of Concord River, said to contain some seventy acres, is a mile southwest; and White Pond, of about forty acres, is a mile and a half beyond

Fair Haven. This is my lake country. These, with Concord River, are my water privileges; and night and day, year in year out, they grind such grist as I carry to them.

Since the wood-cutters, and the railroad, and I myself have profaned Walden, perhaps the most attractive, if not the most beautiful, of all our lakes, the gem of the woods, is White Pond;—a poor name from its commonness, whether derived from the remarkable purity of its waters or the color of its sands. In these as in other respects, however, it is a lesser twin of Walden. They are so much alike that you would say they must be connected under ground. It has the same stony shore, and its waters are of the same hue. As at Walden, in sultry dog-day weather, looking down through the woods on some of its bays which are not so deep but that the reflection from the bottom tinges them, its waters are of a misty bluish-green or glaucous color. Many years since I used to go there to collect the sand by cartloads, to make sandpaper† with, and I have continued to visit it ever since. One who frequents it proposes to call it Virid Lake. Perhaps it might be called Yellow Pine Lake, from the following circumstance. About fifteen years ago you could see the top of a pitch pine, of the kind called yellow pine hereabouts, though it is not a distinct species, projecting above the surface in deep water, many rods from the shore. It was even supposed by some that the pond had sunk, and this was one of the primitive forest that formerly stood there. I find that even so long ago as 1792, in a "Topographical Description of the Town of Concord," by one of its citizens, in the Collections of the Massachusetts Historical Society, the author, after speaking of Walden and White Ponds, adds, "In the middle of the latter may be seen, when the water is very low, a tree which appears as if it grew in the place where it now stands, although the roots are fifty feet below the surface of the water; the top of this tree is broken off, and at that place measures fourteen inches in diameter." In the spring of '49 I talked with the man who lives nearest the pond in Sudbury, who told me that it was he who got out this tree ten or fifteen years before. As near as he could remember, it stood twelve or fifteen rods from the shore, where the water was thirty or forty feet deep. It was in the winter, and he had been getting out ice in the forenoon, and had resolved that in the afternoon, with the aid of his neighbors, he would take out the old yellow pine. He sawed a channel in the ice toward the shore, and hauled it over and along and out on to the ice with oxen; but, before he had gone far in his work, he was surprised to find that it was wrong end upward, with the stumps of the branches pointing down, and the small end firmly fastened in the sandy bottom. It was about a foot in diameter at the big end, and he had expected to get a good saw-log, but it was so rotten as to be fit only for fuel, if for that. He had some of it in his shed then. There were marks of an axe and of woodpeckers on the butt. He thought that it might have been a dead tree on the shore, but was finally blown over into the pond, and after the top had become water-logged, while the butt end was still dry and light, had drifted out and sunk wrong end up. His father, eighty years old, could not remember when it was not there. Several pretty large logs may still be seen lying on the bottom, where, owing to the undulation of the surface, they look like huge water snakes in motion.

This pond has rarely been profaned by a boat, for there is little in it to tempt a fisherman. Instead of the white lily, which requires mud, or the common sweet flag, the blue flag (*Iris versicolor*) grows thinly in the pure water, rising from the stony bottom all around the shore, where it is visited by hummingbirds in June; and the color both of its bluish blades and its flowers and especially their reflections, is in singular harmony with the glaucous water.

White Pond and Walden are great crystals on the surface of the earth, Lakes of Light. If they were permanently congealed, and small enough to be clutched, they would, perchance, be carried off by slaves, like precious stones, to adorn the heads of emperors; but being liquid, and ample, and secured to us and our successors forever, we disregard them, and run after the diamond of Kohinoor.† They are too pure to have a market value; they contain no muck. How much more beautiful than our lives, how much more transparent than our characters, are they! We never learned meanness of them. How much fairer than the pool before the farmer's door, in which his ducks swim! Hither the clean wild ducks come. Nature has no human inhabitant who appreciates her. The birds with their plumage and their notes are in harmony with the flowers, but what youth or maiden conspires with the wild luxuriant beauty of Nature? She flourishes most alone, far from the towns where they reside. Talk of heaven! ye disgrace earth.

From: *Walden*

HIGHER LAWS

As I came home through the woods with my string of fish, trailing my pole, it being now quite dark, I caught a glimpse of a woodchuck stealing across my path, and felt a strange thrill of savage delight, and was strongly tempted to seize and devour him raw; not that I was hungry then, except for that wildness which he represented. Once or twice, however, while I lived at the pond, I found myself ranging the woods, like a half-starved hound, with a strange abandonment, seeking some kind of venison which I might devour, and no morsel could have been too savage for me. The wildest scenes had become unaccountably familiar. I found in myself, and still find, an instinct toward a higher, or, as it is named, spiritual life, as do most men, and another toward a primitive rank and savage one, and I reverence them both. I love the wild not less than the good. The wildness and adventure that are in fishing still recommended it to me. I like sometimes to take rank hold on life and spend my day more as the animals do. Perhaps I have owed to this employment and to hunting, when quite young, my closest acquaintance with Nature. They early introduce us to and detain us in scenery with which otherwise, at that age, we should have little acquaintance. Fishermen, hunters, woodchoppers, and others, spending their lives in the fields and woods, in a peculiar sense a part of Nature themselves, are often in a more favorable mood for observing her, in the intervals of their pursuits, than philosophers or poets even, who approach her with expectation. She is not afraid to exhibit herself to them. The traveller on the prairie is naturally a hunter, on the head waters of the Missouri and Columbia a trapper, and at the Falls of St. Mary a fisherman. He who is only a traveller learns things at second-hand and by the halves, and is poor authority. We are most interested when science reports what those men already know practically or instinctively, for that alone is a true *humanity*, or account of human experience.

They mistake who assert that the Yankee† has few amusements, because he has not so many public holidays, and men and boys do not play so many games as they do in England, for here the more primitive but solitary amusements of hunting, fishing, and the like have not yet given place to the former. Almost every New England boy among my contemporaries shouldered a fowling-piece between the ages of ten and fourteen; and his hunting and fishing grounds were not limited, like the preserves of an English nobleman, but were more boundless even than those of a savage. No wonder, then, that he did not oftener stay to play on the common. But already a change is taking place, owing, not to an increased humanity, but to an increased scarcity of game, for perhaps the hunter is the greatest friend of the animals hunted, not excepting the Humane Society.

Moreover, when at the pond, I wished sometimes to add fish to my fare for variety. I have actually fished from the same kind of necessity that the first fishers did. Whatever humanity I might conjure up against it was all factitious, and concerned my philosophy more than my feelings. I speak of fishing only now, for I had long felt differently about fowling, and sold my gun before I went to the woods. Not that I am less humane than others, but I did not perceive that my feelings were much affected. I did not pity the fishes nor the worms. This was habit. As for fowling, during the last years that I carried a gun my excuse was that I was studying ornithology, and sought only new or rare birds. But I confess that I am now inclined to think that there is a finer way of studying ornithology than this. It requires so much closer attention to the habits of the birds, that, if for that reason only, I have been willing to omit the gun. Yet notwithstanding the objection on the score of humanity, I am compelled to doubt if equally valuable sports are ever substituted for these; and when some of my friends have asked me anxiously about their boys, whether they should let them hunt, I have answered, yes—remembering that it was one of the best parts of my education,—*make* them hunters, though sportsmen only at first, if possible, mighty hunters at last, so that they shall not find game large enough for them in this or any vegetable wilderness,—hunters as well as fishers of men. Thus far I am of the opinion of Chaucer's nun,† who

> "yave not of the text a pulled hen
> That saith that hunters ben not holy men."

There is a period in the history of the individual, as of the race, when the hunters are the "best men," as the Algonquins† called them. We cannot but pity the boy who has never fired a gun; he is no more humane, while his education has been sadly neglected. This was my answer with respect to those youths who were bent on this pursuit, trusting that they would soon outgrow it. No humane being, past the thoughtless age of boyhood, will wantonly murder any creature which holds its life by the same tenure that he does. The hare in its extremity cries like a child. I warn you, mothers, that my sympathies do not always make the usual *philanthropic* distinctions.

Such is oftenest the young man's introduction to the forest, and the most original part of himself. He goes thither at first as a hunter and fisher, until at last, if he has the seeds of a better life in him, he distinguishes his proper objects, as a poet or naturalist it may be, and leaves the gun and fish-pole behind. The mass of men are still and always young in this respect. In some countries a hunting parson is no uncommon sight. Such a one might make a good shepherd's dog, but is far from being the Good Shepherd. I have been surprised to consider that the only obvious employment, except wood-chopping, ice-cutting, or the like business, which ever to my knowledge detained at Walden Pond for a whole half-day any of my fellow-citizens, whether fathers or children of the town, with just one exception, was fishing. Commonly they did not think that they were lucky, or well paid for their time, unless they got a long string of fish, though they had the opportunity of seeing the pond all the while. They might go there a thousand times before the sediment of fishing would sink to the bottom and leave their purpose pure; but no doubt such a clarifying process would be going on all the while. The Governor and his Council faintly remember the pond, for they went a-fishing there when they were boys; but now they are too old and dignified to go a-fishing, and so they know it no more forever. Yet even they expect to go to heaven at last. If the legislature regards it, it is chiefly to regulate the number of hooks to be used there; but they know nothing about the hook of hooks with which to angle for the pond itself, impaling the legislature for a bait. Thus, even in civilized communities, the embryo man passes through the hunter stage of development.

I have found repeatedly, of late years, that I cannot fish without falling a little in self-respect. I have tried it again and again. I have skill at it, and, like many of my fellows, a certain instinct for it, which revives from time to time, but always when I have done I feel that it would have been better if I had not fished. I think that I do not mistake. It is a faint intimation, yet so are the first streaks of morning. There is unquestionably this instinct in me which belongs to the lower orders of creation; yet with every year I am less a fisherman, though without more humanity or even wisdom; at present I am no fisherman at all. But I see that if I were to live in a wilderness I should again be tempted to become a fisher and hunter in earnest. Beside, there is something essentially unclean about this diet and all flesh, and I began to see where house-work commences, and whence the endeavor, which costs so much, to wear a tidy and respectable appearance each day, to keep the house sweet and free from all ill odors and sights. Having been my own butcher and scullion and cook, as well as the gentleman for whom the dishes were served up, I can speak from an unusually complete experience. The practical objection to animal food in my case was its uncleanness; and besides, when I had caught and cleaned and cooked and eaten my fish, they seemed not to have fed me essentially. It was insignificant and unnecessary, and cost more than it came to. A little bread or a few potatoes would have done as well, with less trouble and filth. Like many of my contemporaries, I had rarely for many years used animal food, or tea, or coffee, etc.; not so much because of any ill effects which I had traced to them, as because they were not agreeable to my imagination. The repugnance to animal food is not the effect of experience, but is an instinct. It appeared more beautiful to live low and fare hard in many respects; and though I never did so, I went far enough to please my imagination. I believe that every man who has ever been earnest to preserve his higher or poetic faculties in the best condition has been particularly inclined to abstain from animal food, and from much food of any kind. It is a significant fact, stated by entomologists,—I find it in Kirby and Spence,[†]— that "some insects in their perfect state, though furnished with organs of feeding, make no use of them:" and they lay it down as "a general rule, that almost all insects in this state eat much less than in that of larvae. The voracious caterpillar when transformed into a butterfly ... and the gluttonous maggot when become a fly" content themselves with a drop or two of honey or some other sweet liquid. The abdomen under the wings of the butterfly still represents the larva. This is the tidbit which tempts his insectivorous fate. The gross feeder is a man in the larva state; and there are whole nations in that condition, nations without fancy or imagination, whose vast abdomens betray them.

It is hard to provide and cook so simple and clean a diet as will not offend the imagination; but this, I think, is to be fed when we feed the body; they should both sit down at the same table. Yet perhaps this may be done. The fruits eaten temperately need not make us ashamed of our appetites, nor interrupt the worthiest pursuits. But put an extra condiment into your dish, and it will poison you. It is not worth the while to live by rich cookery. Most men would feel shame if caught preparing with their own hands precisely such a dinner, whether of animal or vegetable food, as is every day prepared for them by others. Yet till this is otherwise we are not civilized, and, if gentlemen and ladies, are not true men and women. This certainly suggests what change is to be made. It may be vain to ask why the imagination will not be reconciled to flesh and fat. I am satisfied that it is not. Is it not a reproach that man is a carnivorous animal? True, he can and does live, in a great measure, by preying on other animals; but this is a miserable way,—as any one who will go to snaring rabbits, or slaughtering lambs, may learn,—and he will be regarded as a benefactor of his race who shall teach man to confine himself to a more innocent and wholesome diet. Whatever my own practice may be, I have no doubt that it is a part of the destiny of the human race, in its gradual improvement, to leave off eating animals, as surely as the savage tribes have left off eating each other when they came in contact with the more civilized.

If one listens to the faintest but constant suggestions of his genius, which are certainly true, he sees not to what extremes, or even insanity, it may lead him; and yet that way, as he grows more resolute and faithful, his road lies. The faintest assured objection which one healthy man feels will at length prevail over the arguments and customs of mankind. No man ever followed his genius till it misled him. Though the result were bodily weakness, yet perhaps no one can say that the consequences were to be regretted, for these were a life in conformity to higher principles. If the day and the night are such that you greet them with joy, and life emits a fragrance like flowers and sweet-scented herbs, is more elastic, more starry, more immortal,—that is your success. All nature is your congratulation, and you have cause momentarily to bless yourself. The greatest gains and values are farthest from being appreciated. We easily come to doubt if they exist. We soon forget them. They are the highest reality. Perhaps the facts most astounding and most real are never communicated by man to man. The true harvest of my daily life is somewhat as intangible and indescribable as the tints of morning or evening. It is a little star-dust caught, a segment of the rainbow which I have clutched.

Yet, for my part, I was never unusually squeamish; I could sometimes eat a fried rat with a good relish, if it were necessary. I am glad to have drunk water so long, for the same reason that I prefer the natural sky to an opium-eater's heaven. I would fain keep sober always; and there are infinite degrees of drunkenness. I believe that water is the only drink for a wise man: wine is not so noble a liquor; and think of dashing the hopes of a morning with a cup of warm coffee, or of an evening with a dish of tea! Ah, how low I fall when I am tempted by them! Even music may be intoxicating. Such apparently slight causes destroyed Greece and Rome, and will destroy England and America. Of all ebriosity, who does not prefer to be intoxicated by the air he breathes? I have found it to be the most serious objection to coarse labors long continued, that they compelled me to eat and drink coarsely also. But to tell the truth, I find myself at present somewhat less particular in these respects. I carry less religion to the table, ask no blessing; not because I am wiser than I was, but, I am obliged to confess, because, however much it is to be regretted, with years I have grown more coarse and indifferent. Perhaps these questions are entertained only in youth, as most believe of poetry.

My practice is "nowhere," my opinion is here. Nevertheless I am far from regarding myself as one of those privileged ones to whom the Ved† refers when it says, that "he who has true faith in the Omnipresent Supreme Being may eat all that exists," that is, is not bound to inquire what is his food, or who prepares it; and even in their case it is to be observed, as a Hindoo commentator† has remarked, that the Vedant limits this privilege to "the time of distress."

Who has not sometimes derived an inexpressible satisfaction from his food in which appetite had no share? I have been thrilled to think that I owed a mental perception to the commonly gross sense of taste, that I have been inspired through the palate, that some berries which I had eaten on a hillside had fed my genius. "The soul not being mistress of herself," says Thseng-tseu,† "one looks, and one does not see; one listens, and one does not hear; one eats, and one does not know the savor of food." He who distinguishes the true savor of his food can never be a glutton; he who does not cannot be otherwise. A puritan may go to his brown-bread crust with as gross an appetite as ever an alderman to his turtle. Not that food which entereth into the mouth defileth a man, but the appetite with which it is eaten. It is neither the quality nor the quantity, but the devotion to sensual savors; when that which is eaten is not a viand to sustain our animal, or inspire our spiritual life, but food for the worms that possess us. If the hunter has a taste for mud-turtles, muskrats, and other such savage tidbits, the fine lady indulges a taste for jelly made of a calf's foot, or for sardines from over the sea, and they are even. He goes to the mill-pond, she to her preserve-pot. The wonder is how they, how you and I, can live this slimy, beastly life, eating and drinking.

Our whole life is startlingly moral. There is never an instant's truce between virtue and vice. Goodness is the only investment that never fails. In the music of the harp which trembles round the world it is the insisting on this which thrills us. The harp is the travelling patterer for the Universe's Insurance Company, recommending its laws, and our little goodness is all the assessment that we pay. Though the youth at last grows indifferent, the laws of the universe are not indifferent, but are forever on the side of the most sensitive. Listen to every zephyr for some reproof, for it is surely there, and he is unfortunate who does not hear it. We cannot touch a string or move a stop but the charming moral transfixes us. Many an irksome noise, go a long way off, is heard as music, a proud, sweet satire on the meanness of our lives.

We are conscious of an animal in us, which awakens in proportion as our higher nature slumbers. It is reptile and sensual, and perhaps cannot be wholly expelled; like the worms which, even in life and health, occupy our bodies. Possibly we may withdraw from it, but never change its nature. I fear that it may enjoy a certain health of its own; that we may be well, yet not pure. The other day I picked up the lower jaw of a hog, with white and sound teeth and tusks, which suggested that there was an animal health and vigor distinct from the spiritual. This creature succeeded by other means than temperance and purity. "That in which men differ from brute beasts," says Mencius,† "is a thing very inconsiderable; the common herd lose it very soon; superior men preserve it carefully." Who knows what sort of life would result if we had attained to purity? If I knew so wise a man as could teach me purity I would go to seek him forthwith. "A command over our passions, and over the external senses of the body, and good acts, are declared by the Ved to be indispensable in the mind's approximation to God." Yet the spirit can for the time pervade and control every member and function of the body, and transmute what in form is the grossest sensuality into purity and devotion. The generative energy, which, when we are loose, dissipates and makes us unclean, when we are continent invigorates and inspires us. Chastity is the flowering of man; and what are called Genius, Heroism, Holiness, and the like, are but various fruits which succeed it. Man flows at once to God when the channel of purity is open. By turns our purity inspires and our impurity casts us down. He is blessed who is assured that the animal is dying out in him day by day, and the divine being established. Perhaps there is none but has cause for shame on account of the inferior and brutish nature to which he is allied. I fear that we are such gods or demigods only as fauns and satyrs, the divine allied to beasts, the creatures of appetite, and that, to some extent, our very life is our disgrace. —

> "How happy's he who hath due place assigned
> To his beasts and disafforested his mind!
> * * * * * * * * *
> Can use this horse, goat, wolf, and ev'ry beast,
> And is not ass himself to all the rest!
> Else man not only is the herd of swine,
> But he's those devils too which did incline
> Them to a headlong rage, and made them worse."†

All sensuality is one, though it takes many forms; all purity is one. It is the same whether a man eat, or drink, or cohabit, or sleep sensually. They are but one appetite, and we only need to see a person do any one of these things to know how great a sensualist he is. The impure can neither stand nor sit with purity. When the reptile is attacked at one mouth of his burrow, he shows himself at another. If you would be chaste, you must be temperate. What is chastity? How shall a man know if he is chaste? He shall not know it. We have heard of this virtue, but we know not what it is. We speak conformably to the rumor which we have heard. From exertion come wisdom and purity; from sloth ignorance and sensuality. In the student sensuality is a sluggish habit of mind. An unclean person is universally a slothful one, one who sits by a stove, whom the sun shines on prostrate, who reposes without being fatigued. If you would avoid uncleanness, and all the sins, work earnestly, though it be at cleaning a stable. Nature is hard to be overcome, but she must be overcome. What avails it that you are Christian, if you are not purer than the heathen, if you deny yourself no more, if you are not more religious? I know of many systems of religion esteemed heathenish whose precepts fill the reader with shame, and provoke him to new endeavors, though it be to the performance of rites merely.

I hesitate to say these things, but it is not because of the subject,—I care not how obscene my *words* are,—but because I cannot speak of them without betraying my impurity. We discourse freely without shame of one form of sensuality, and are silent about another. We are so degraded that we cannot speak simply of the necessary functions of human nature. In earlier ages, in some countries, every function was reverently spoken of and regulated by law. Nothing was too trivial for the Hindoo lawgiver, however offensive it may be to modern taste. He teaches how to eat, drink, cohabit, void excrement and urine, and the like, elevating what is mean, and does not falsely excuse himself by calling these things trifles.

Every man is the builder of a temple, called his body, to the god he worships, after a style purely his own, nor can he get off by hammering marble instead. We are all sculptors and painters, and our material is our own flesh and blood and bones. Any nobleness begins at once to refine a man's features, any meanness or sensuality to imbrute them.

John Farmer sat at his door one September evening, after a hard day's work, his mind still running on his labor more or less. Having bathed, he sat down to re-create his intellectual man. It was a rather cool evening, and some of his neighbors were apprehending a frost. He had not attended to the train of his thoughts long when he heard some one playing on a flute, and that sound harmonized with his mood. Still he thought of his work; but the burden of his thought was, that though this kept running in his head, and he found himself planning and contriving it against his will, yet it concerned him very little. It was no more than the scurf of his skin, which was constantly shuffled off. But the notes of the flute came home to his ears out of a different sphere from that he worked in, and suggested work for certain faculties which slumbered in him. They gently did away with the street, and the village, and the state in which he lived. A voice said to him,—Why do you stay here and live this mean moiling life, when a glorious existence is possible for you? Those same stars twinkle over other fields than these.—But how to come out of this condition and actually migrate thither? All that he could think of was to practise some new austerity, to let his mind descend into his body and redeem it, and treat himself with ever increasing respect.

From: *Walden*

CONCLUSION

TO THE SICK the doctors wisely recommend a change of air and scenery. Thank Heaven, here is not all the world. The buckeye does not grow in New England, and the mockingbird is rarely heard here. The wild goose is more of a cosmopolite than we; he breaks his fast in Canada, takes a luncheon in the Ohio, and plumes himself for the night in a southern bayou. Even the bison, to some extent, keeps pace with the seasons cropping the pastures of the Colorado only till a greener and sweeter grass awaits him by the Yellowstone.† Yet we think that if rail fences are pulled down, and stone walls piled up on our farms, bounds are henceforth set to our lives and our fates decided. If you are chosen town clerk, forsooth, you cannot go to Tierra del Fuego† this summer: but you may go to the land of infernal fire nevertheless. The universe is wider than our views of it.

Yet we should oftener look over the tafferel of our craft, like curious passengers, and not make the voyage like stupid sailors picking oakum. The other side of the globe is but the home of our correspondent. Our voyaging is only great-circle sailing, and the doctors prescribe for diseases of the skin merely. One hastens to southern Africa to chase the giraffe; but surely that is not the game he would be after. How long, pray, would a man hunt giraffes if he could? Snipes and woodcocks also may afford rare sport; but I trust it would be nobler game to shoot one's self.—

> "Direct your eye sight inward, and you'll find
> A thousand regions in your mind
> Yet undiscovered. Travel them, and be
> Expert in home-cosmography."†

What does Africa,—what does the West stand for? Is not our own interior white on the chart? black though it may prove, like the coast, when discovered. Is it the source of the Nile, or the Niger, or the Mississippi, or a Northwest Passage[†] around this continent, that we would find? Are these the problems which most concern mankind? Is Franklin[†] the only man who is lost, that his wife should be so earnest to find him? Does Mr. Grinnell[†] know where he himself is? Be rather the Mungo Park,[†] the Lewis and Clark[†] and Frobisher,[†] of your own streams and oceans; explore your own higher latitudes,—with shiploads of preserved meats to support you, if they be necessary; and pile the empty cans sky-high for a sign. Were preserved meats invented to preserve meat merely? Nay, be a Columbus to whole new continents and worlds within you, opening new channels, not of trade, but of thought. Every man is the lord of a realm beside which the earthly empire of the Czar is but a petty state, a hummock left by the ice. Yet some can be patriotic who have no *self*-respect, and sacrifice the greater to the less. They love the soil which makes their graves, but have no sympathy with the spirit which may still animate their clay. Patriotism is a maggot in their heads. What was the meaning of that South-Sea Exploring Expedition,[†] with all its parade and expense, but an indirect recognition of the fact that there are continents and seas in the moral world to which every man is an isthmus or an inlet, yet unexplored by him, but that it is easier to sail many thousand miles through cold and storm and cannibals, in a government ship, with five hundred men and boys to assist one, than it is to explore the private sea, the Atlantic and Pacific Ocean of one's being alone.

> "Erret, et extremos alter scrutetur Iberos.
> Plus habet hic vitae, plus habet ille viae."

> Let them wander and scrutinize the outlandish Australians.
> I have more of God, they more of the road.[†]

It is not worth the while to go round the world to count the cats in Zanzibar.[†] Yet do this even till you can do better, and you may perhaps find some "Symmes' Hole"[†] by which to get at the inside at last. England and France, Spain and Portugal, Gold Coast and Slave Coast,[†] all front on this private sea; but no bark from them has ventured out of sight of land, though it is without doubt the direct way to India. If you would learn to speak all tongues and conform to the customs of all nations, if you would travel farther than all travellers, be naturalized in all climes, and cause the Sphinx[†] to dash her head against a stone, even obey the precept of the old philosopher, and Explore thyself. Herein are demanded the eye and the nerve. Only the defeated and deserters go to the wars, cowards that run away and enlist. Start now on that farthest western way, which does not pause at the Mississippi or the Pacific, nor conduct toward a worn-out China or Japan, but leads on direct, a tangent to this sphere, summer and winter, day and night, sun down, moon down, and at last earth down too.

It is said that Mirabeau† took to highway robbery "to ascertain what degree of resolution was necessary in order to place one's self in formal opposition to the most sacred laws of society." He declared that "a soldier who fights in the ranks does not require half so much courage as a foot-pad,"—"that honor and religion have never stood in the way of a well-considered and a firm resolve." This was manly, as the world goes; and yet it was idle, if not desperate. A saner man would have found himself often enough "in formal opposition" to what are deemed "the most sacred laws of society," through obedience to yet more sacred laws, and so have tested his resolution without going out of his way. It is not for a man to put himself in such an attitude to society, but to maintain himself in whatever attitude he find himself through obedience to the laws of his being, which will never be one of opposition to a just government, if he should chance to meet with such.

I left the woods for as good a reason as I went there. Perhaps it seemed to me that I had several more lives to live, and could not spare any more time for that one. It is remarkable how easily and insensibly we fall into a particular route, and make a beaten track for ourselves. I had not lived there a week before my feet wore a path from my door to the pond-side; and though it is five or six years since I trod it, it is still quite distinct. It is true, I fear, that others may have fallen into it, and so helped to keep it open. The surface of the earth is soft and impressible by the feet of men; and so with the paths which the mind travels. How worn and dusty, then, must be the highways of the world, how deep the ruts of tradition and conformity! I did not wish to take a cabin passage, but rather to go before the mast and on the deck of the world, for there I could best see the moonlight amid the mountains. I do not wish to go below now.

I learned this, at least, by my experiment: that if one advances confidently in the direction of his dreams, and endeavors to live the life which he has imagined, he will meet with a success unexpected in common hours. He will put some things behind, will pass an invisible boundary; new, universal, and more liberal laws will begin to establish themselves around and within him; or the old laws be expanded, and interpreted in his favor in a more liberal sense, and he will live with the license of a higher order of beings. In proportion as he simplifies his life, the laws of the universe will appear less complex, and solitude will not be solitude, nor poverty poverty, nor weakness weakness. If you have built castles in the air, your work need not be lost; that is where they should be. Now put the foundations under them.

It is a ridiculous demand which England and America make, that you shall speak so that they can understand you. Neither men nor toadstools grow so. As if that were important, and there were not enough to understand you without them. As if Nature could support but one order of understandings, could not sustain birds as well as quadrupeds, flying as well as creeping things, and *hush* and *whoa*, which Bright can understand, were the best English. As if there were safety in stupidity alone. I fear chiefly lest my expression may not be extra-vagant enough, may not wander far enough beyond the narrow limits of my daily experience, so as to be adequate to the truth of which I have been convinced. *Extra vagance!* it depends on how you are yarded. The migrating buffalo, which seeks new pastures in another latitude, is not extravagant like the cow which kicks over the pail, leaps the cowyard fence, and runs after her calf, in milking time. I desire to speak somewhere *without* bounds; like a man in a waking moment, to men in their waking moments; for I am convinced that I cannot exaggerate enough even to lay the foundation of a true expression. Who that has heard a strain of music feared then lest he should speak extravagantly any more forever? In view of the future or possible, we should live quite laxly and undefined in front, our outlines dim and misty on that side; as our shadows reveal an insensible perspiration toward the sun. The volatile truth of our words should continually betray the inadequacy of the residual statement. Their truth is instantly *translated*; its literal monument alone remains. The words which express our faith and piety are not definite; yet they are significant and fragrant like frankincense to superior natures.

Why level downward to our dullest perception always, and praise that as common sense? The commonest sense is the sense of men asleep, which they express by snoring. Sometimes we are inclined to class those who are once-and-a-half-witted with the half-witted, because we appreciate only a third part of their wit. Some would find fault with the morning red, if they ever got up early enough. "They pretend," as I hear, "that the verses of Kabir[†] have four different senses; illusion, spirit, intellect, and the exoteric doctrine of the Vedas"; but in this part of the world it is considered a ground for complaint if a man's writings admit of more than one interpretation. While England endeavors to cure the potato-rot, will not any endeavor to cure the brain-rot, which prevails so much more widely and fatally?

I do not suppose that I have attained to obscurity, but I should be proud if no more fatal fault were found with my pages on this score than was found with the Walden ice. Southern customers objected to its blue color, which is the evidence of its purity, as if it were muddy, and preferred the Cambridge ice, which is white, but tastes of weeds. The purity men love is like the mists which envelop the earth, and not like the azure ether beyond.

Some are dinning in our ears that we Americans, and moderns generally, are intellectual dwarfs compared with the ancients, or even the Elizabethan men. But what is that to the purpose? A living dog is better than a dead lion.† Shall a man go and hang himself because he belongs to the race of pygmies, and not be the biggest pygmy that he can? Let every one mind his own business, and endeavor to be what he was made.

Why should we be in such desperate haste to succeed and in such desperate enterprises? If a man does not keep pace with his companions, perhaps it is because he hears a different drummer. Let him step to the music which he hears, however measured or far away. It is not important that he should mature as soon as an apple tree or an oak. Shall he turn his spring into summer? If the condition of things which we were made for is not yet, what were any reality which we can substitute? We will not be shipwrecked on a vain reality. Shall we with pains erect a heaven of blue glass over ourselves, though when it is done we shall be sure to gaze still at the true ethereal heaven far above, as if the former were not?

There was an artist in the city of Kouroo who was disposed to strive after perfection. One day it came into his mind to make a staff. Having considered that in an imperfect work time is an ingredient, but into a perfect work time does not enter, he said to himself, It shall be perfect in all respects, though I should do nothing else in my life. He proceeded instantly to the forest for wood, being resolved that it should not be made of unsuitable material; and as he searched for and rejected stick after stick, his friends gradually deserted him, for they grew old in their works and died, but he grew not older by a moment. His singleness of purpose and resolution, and his elevated piety, endowed him, without his knowledge, with perennial youth. As he made no compromise with Time, Time kept out of his way, and only sighed at a distance because he could not overcome him. Before he had found a stock in all respects suitable the city of Kouroo was a hoary ruin, and he sat on one of its mounds to peel the stick. Before he had given it the proper shape the dynasty of the Candahars was at an end, and with the point of the stick he wrote the name of the last of that race in the sand, and then resumed his work. By the time he had smoothed and polished the staff Kalpa was no longer the pole-star; and ere he had put on the ferule and the head adorned with precious stones, Brahma had awoke and slumbered many times. But why do I stay to mention these things? When the finishing stroke was put to his work, it suddenly expanded before the eyes of the astonished artist into the fairest of all the creations of Brahma. He had made a new system in making a staff, a world with full and fair proportions; in which, though the old cities and dynasties had passed away, fairer and more glorious ones had taken their places. And now he saw by the heap of shavings still fresh at his feet, that, for him and his work, the former lapse of time had been an illusion, and that no more time had elapsed than is required for a single scintillation from the brain of Brahma to fall on and inflame the tinder of a mortal brain. The material was pure, and his art was pure; how could the result be other than wonderful?

No face which we can give to a matter will stead us so well at last as the truth. This alone wears well. For the most part, we are not where we are, but in a false position. Through an infirmity of our natures, we suppose a case, and put ourselves into it, and hence are in two cases at the same time, and it is doubly difficult to get out. In sane moments we regard only the facts, the case that is. Say what you have to say, not what you ought. Any truth is better than make-believe. Tom Hyde, the tinker, standing on the gallows, was asked if he had anything to say. "Tell the tailors," said he, "to remember to make a knot in their thread before they take the first stitch." His companion's prayer is forgotten.

However mean your life is, meet it and live it; do not shun it and call it hard names. It is not so bad as you are. It looks poorest when you are richest. The fault-finder will find faults even in paradise. Love your life, poor as it is. You may perhaps have some pleasant, thrilling, glorious hours, even in a poor-house. The setting sun is reflected from the windows of the almshouse as brightly as from the rich man's abode; the snow melts before its door as early in the spring. I do not see but a quiet mind may live as contentedly there, and have as cheering thoughts, as in a palace. The town's poor seem to me often to live the most independent lives of any. Maybe they are simply great enough to receive without misgiving. Most think that they are above being supported by the town; but it oftener happens that they are not above supporting themselves by dishonest means, which should be more disreputable. Cultivate poverty like a garden herb, like sage. Do not trouble yourself much to get new things, whether clothes or friends. Turn the old; return to them. Things do not change; we change. Sell your clothes and keep your thoughts. God will see that you do not want society. If I were confined to a corner of a garret all my days, like a spider, the world would be just as large to me while I had my thoughts about me. The philosopher said: "From an army of three divisions one can take away its general, and put it in disorder; from the man the most abject and vulgar one cannot take away his thought." Do not seek so anxiously to be developed, to subject yourself to many influences to be played on; it is all dissipation. Humility like darkness reveals the heavenly lights. The shadows of poverty and meanness gather around us, "and lo! creation widens to our view."† We are often reminded that if there were bestowed on us the wealth of Croesus,† our aims must still be the same, and our means essentially the same. Moreover, if you are restricted in your range by poverty, if you cannot buy books and newspapers, for instance, you are but confined to the most significant and vital experiences; you are compelled to deal with the material which yields the most sugar and the most starch. It is life near the bone where it is sweetest. You are defended from being a trifler. No man loses ever on a lower level by magnanimity on a higher. Superfluous wealth can buy superfluities only. Money is not required to buy one necessary of the soul.

I live in the angle of a leaden wall, into whose composition was poured a little alloy of bell-metal. Often, in the repose of my mid-day, there reaches my ears a confused *tintinnabulum* from without. It is the noise of my contemporaries. My neighbors tell me of their adventures with famous gentlemen and ladies, what notabilities they met at the dinner-table; but I am no more interested in such things than in the contents of the Daily Times. The interest and the conversation are about costume and manners chiefly; but a goose is a goose still, dress it as you will. They tell me of California and Texas, of England and the Indies, of the Hon. Mr.—of Georgia or of Massachusetts, all transient and fleeting phenomena, till I am ready to leap from their court-yard like the Mameluke bey.† I delight to come to my bearings,—not walk in procession with pomp and parade, in a conspicuous place, but to walk even with the Builder of the universe, if I may,—not to live in this restless, nervous, bustling, trivial Nineteenth Century, but stand or sit thoughtfully while it goes by. What are men celebrating? They are all on a committee of arrangements, and hourly expect a speech from somebody. God is only the president of the day, and Webster† is his orator. I love to weigh, to settle, to gravitate toward that which most strongly and rightfully attracts me;—not hang by the beam of the scale and try to weigh less,—not suppose a case, but take the case that is; to travel the only path I can, and that on which no power can resist me. It affords me no satisfaction to commence to spring an arch before I have got a solid foundation. Let us not play at kittly-benders. There is a solid bottom everywhere. We read that the traveller asked the boy if the swamp before him had a hard bottom. The boy replied that it had. But presently the traveller's horse sank in up to the girths, and he observed to the boy, "I thought you said that this bog had a hard bottom." "So it has," answered the latter, "but you have not got half way to it yet." So it is with the bogs and quicksands of society; but he is an old boy that knows it. Only what is thought, said, or done at a certain rare coincidence is good. I would not be one of those who will foolishly drive a nail into mere lath and plastering; such a deed would keep me awake nights. Give me a hammer, and let me feel for the furring. Do not depend on the putty. Drive a nail home and clinch it so faithfully that you can wake up in the night and think of your work with satisfaction,—a work at which you would not be ashamed to invoke the Muse. So will help you God, and so only. Every nail driven should be as another rivet in the machine of the universe, you carrying on the work.

Rather than love, than money, than fame, give me truth. I sat at a table where were rich food and wine in abundance, and obsequious attendance, but sincerity and truth were not; and I went away hungry from the inhospitable board. The hospitality was as cold as the ices. I thought that there was no need of ice to freeze them. They talked to me of the age of the wine and the fame of the vintage; but I thought of an older, a newer, and purer wine, of a more glorious vintage, which they had not got, and could not buy. The style, the house and grounds and "entertainment" pass for nothing with me. I called on the king, but he made me wait in his hall, and conducted like a man incapacitated for hospitality. There was a man in my neighborhood who lived in a hollow tree. His manners were truly regal. I should have done better had I called on him.

How long shall we sit in our porticoes practising idle and musty virtues, which any work would make impertinent? As if one were to begin the day with long-suffering, and hire a man to hoe his potatoes; and in the afternoon go forth to practise Christian meekness and charity with goodness aforethought! Consider the China pride and stagnant self-complacency of mankind. This generation inclines a little to congratulate itself on being the last of an illustrious line; and in Boston and London and Paris and Rome, thinking of its long descent, it speaks of its progress in art and science and literature with satisfaction. There are the Records of the Philosophical Societies, and the public Eulogies of *Great Men*! It is the good Adam[†] contemplating his own virtue. "Yes, we have done great deeds, and sung divine songs, which shall never die,"—that is, as long as *we* can remember them. The learned societies and great men of Assyria,—where are they? What youthful philosophers and experimentalists we are! There is not one of my readers who has yet lived a whole human life. These may be but the spring months in the life of the race. If we have had the seven-years' itch, we have not seen the seventeen-year locust yet in Concord. We are acquainted with a mere pellicle of the globe on which we live. Most have not delved six feet beneath the surface, nor leaped as many above it. We know not where we are. Beside, we are sound asleep nearly half our time. Yet we esteem ourselves wise, and have an established order on the surface. Truly, we are deep thinkers, we are ambitious spirits! As I stand over the insect crawling amid the pine needles on the forest floor, and endeavoring to conceal itself from my sight, and ask myself why it will cherish those humble thoughts, and hide its head from me who might, perhaps, be its benefactor, and impart to its race some cheering information, I am reminded of the greater Benefactor and Intelligence that stands over me the human insect.

There is an incessant influx of novelty into the world, and yet we tolerate incredible dulness. I need only suggest what kind of sermons are still listened to in the most enlightened countries. There are such words as joy and sorrow, but they are only the burden of a psalm, sung with a nasal twang, while we believe in the ordinary and mean. We think that we can change our clothes only. It is said that the British Empire is very large and respectable, and that the United States are a first-rate power. We do not believe that a tide rises and falls behind every man which can float the British Empire like a chip, if he should ever harbor it in his mind. Who knows what sort of seventeen-year locust will next come out of the ground? The government of the world I live in was not framed, like that of Britain, in after-dinner conversations over the wine.

The life in us is like the water in the river. It may rise this year higher than man has ever known it, and flood the parched uplands; even this may be the eventful year, which will drown out all our muskrats. It was not always dry land where we dwell. I see far inland the banks which the stream anciently washed, before science began to record its freshets. Every one has heard the story which has gone the rounds of New England, of a strong and beautiful bug which came out of the dry leaf of an old table of apple-tree wood, which had stood in a farmer's kitchen for sixty years, first in Connecticut, and afterward in Massachusetts,—from an egg deposited in the living tree many years earlier still, as appeared by counting the annual layers beyond it; which was heard gnawing out for several weeks, hatched perchance by the heat of an urn. Who does not feel his faith in a resurrection and immortality strengthened by hearing of this? Who knows what beautiful and winged life, whose egg has been buried for ages under many concentric layers of woodenness in the dead dry life of society, deposited at first in the alburnum of the green and living tree, which has been gradually converted into the semblance of its well-seasoned tomb,—heard perchance gnawing out now for years by the astonished family of man, as they sat round the festive board,—may unexpectedly come forth from amidst society's most trivial and handselled furniture, to enjoy its perfect summer life at last!

I do not say that John or Jonathan will realize all this; but such is the character of that morrow which mere lapse of time can never make to dawn. The light which puts out our eyes is darkness to us. Only that day dawns to which we are awake. There is more day to dawn. The sun is but a morning star.

Walden: Where I Lived, and What I Lived For

Glossary

"I am monarch…to dispute." – from eighteenth-century poet William Cowper's "Verses Supposed to be Written by Alexander Selkirk" (1782); this poem has a few other names, including "The Solitude of Alexander Selkirk."

Atlas – a figure from classical mythology who holds the world on his shoulders

Old Cato – Marcus Porcius Cato (243-149 B.C.), now known as Cato the Elder, was a Roman statesman known for his simple living and high moral standards.

"De Re Rustica" – (also called "De Agri Cultura") Roman author Lucius Iunius Moderatus Columell's (4-ca.70 A.D.) manual on farming

Cultivator – a farm journal

Olympus – According to classical mythology, the home of the gods was on Mount Olympus.

Harivansa – an important piece of classical Indian literature dealing with the life of the god Krishna (see later Note, *Damodara*)

Concord Battle Ground – one site of the Battle of Lexington and Concord, the first military engagement in the Revolutionary War

"steppes of Tartary" – a reference to a series of treeless, semi-arid plateaus in Central Asia

Damodara – one of the many names of Krishna, the major Hindu god; often depicted as a young cowherd playing a flute, Damodara is known as a heroic warrior and teacher, and is a central figure in the *Harivansa* (see earlier Note, *Harivansa*).

Cassiopeia's Chair – a constellation in the sky comprised of five stars that make a rough M or W; the ancient Greeks believed it represented a queen in her throne who boasted about her beauty.

Pleiades – a star cluster located in the constellation Taurus; it is also called the Seven Sisters. The constellation is important to many cultures, and it is referred to in many religious and ancient texts.

Hyades – a cluster of stars in the constellation Taurus; the brightest stars form a V. It is the nearest star cluster to Earth.

Aldebaran – one of the brightest stars in the sky; it is in the constellation Taurus.

Altair – another very bright star

"There was a shepherd...feed him by." – from an anonymous sixteenth-century song; Thoreau wonders about the shepherd's philosophy.

Aurora – the goddess of the dawn, according to Roman mythology

King Tching-thang – (1675-1646 B.C.), first king of the Shang Dynasty in China

Homer – (ca. 800-750 B.C.), the blind poet who composed the epic poems, the *Iliad* and the *Odyssey*; exact authorship is unknown, but it is assumed to be Homer, although cases have been made for others, including, in modern times, an unknown woman.

Iliad and Odyssey – epic Greek poems about the Trojan War (*Iliad*) and Ulysses'/Odysseus' return to Greece (*Odyssey*) after the defeat of Troy

The Vedas – the ancient scriptural texts of Hinduism

Memnon – According to Greek mythology, Memnon, a king of Ethiopia, was the son of Aurora, the goddess of the morning, and the mortal man Tithonus.

Spartan-like – The Spartans, residents of Sparta, a city-state in ancient Greece, were famous and feared for their physical endurance and discipline.

"glorify God and enjoy him forever" – This is the main purpose of human life, according to the *Westminster Shorter Catechism,* an important Protestant document.

pygmies...cranes – a reference to an epic simile in Book III of Homer's *Iliad*

dead reckoning – a method of navigation that uses guesses, estimates, and past navigation, rather than precise figures, to locate an exact target; sailing this way was very dangerous and was replaced by accurate instruments like the sextant and, later, radar, as soon as they became available. In this section, Thoreau is comparing a nineteenth-century "modern" life with its numerous dangers and distractions to a ship sailing without direction.

German Confederacy – a group of many small states which were constantly fighting one another; Germany was not united until 1871.

telegraph – a communications system considered modern in Thoreau's day; it transmitted electric impulses in Morse Code through wires.

Saint Vitus' dance – another name for Sydenham's Chorea, a disease characterized by rapid, jerky, involuntary, and uncontrollable movements of the body

Don Carlos...and Granada – This is a reference to political issues in Spain and Portugal during the 1830s and 1840s. Thoreau is continuing to state his opinion that "news" is unnecessary, as is the post office; contemporary events and the yearning for this type of information leads people away from what is more important.

Brahme – Brahme or Brahma is the Hindu god of creation, the essential spirit of Hinduism.

Ulysses – the Roman name for Odysseus, the central figure in Homer's *Odyssey*; he tied himself to his ship's mast so he could hear the lure of the hypnotic Sirens, but could not go to them and be doomed.

a point d'appui – *[French]* a point of support

Nilometer – a device used to measure the water level of the Nile River

cimeter – *[scimitar]* a sword with a long, curved blade

The Village

Etesian – summer winds that pass over the Mediterranean and Aegean Seas that indicate favorable sailing

caryatides – supporting columns that are in the shape of a female figure

Orpheus – See earlier Note, *Orpheus*, in *Civil Disobedience.*

the Sirens – According to Greek mythology, the Sirens were a group of creatures, half-monster, half-women, who sang so beautifully that they lured mariners to destruction on the rocks that surrounded their island. See earlier Note, *Ulysses*, in *Where I Lived, and What I Lived For*

"elsewhere related" – Thoreau discussed the circumstances of arrest in *Civil Disobedience*.

The Pope's – a reference to Alexander Pope (1688-1744), an English poet and satirist, who used heroic couplets to translate Homer's *Iliad* and *Odyssey.*

"You who govern...bends" – an excerpt from Confucius' *Analects*

The Ponds

"fresh woods and pastures new" – from *Lycidas* by John Milton (1608-1674), the English poet.

Coenobites – Coenobites (pronounced "see no bites") were part of a religious community; it is a pun related to the man's fishing.

Michael Angelo – Michelangelo di Lodovico Buonarroti Simoni (1475-1564), was a major Italian sculptor, painter, architect, and poet.

Castalian Fountain – According to Greek mythology, it is a source of poetic inspiration and is sacred to the Muses; the fountain is supposedly located at the summit of Mount Parnassus.

alto relievo – [*Latin*] "high-relief"; an ancient sculptural form used to represent humans and animals in an exaggerated dimensional form

the Revolution – a reference to the American Revolutionary War (1775-1783), when the Colonies rebelled against the British Empire for independence

Muse – See earlier Note, *Muses*, in *Friendship* Glossary.

the Ganges – a major river that flows through northern India into Bangladesh; it is sacred to practitioners of Hinduism.

State Street – Boston's financial district

One – a reference to Emerson, who had suggested the name, "God's Drop" for Walden Pond

Icarian Sea – part of the Aegean Sea, possibly named after Icarus, who, according to Greek mythology, flew too close to the sun with wings made from feathers and wax; the wings melted and he drowned at sea while his father, Daedalus, watched.

"brave attempt resounds" – a reference to the poem *Icarus* by William Drummond of Hawthornden (1585-1649), a Scottish poet

"make sandpaper" – The Thoreau family made sandpaper and pencils.

diamond of Kohinoor – According to legend, the person who possesses this diamond rules the world.

Higher Laws

Yankee – a slang and derogatory term for an American from the North; it achieved great popularity during and after the Civil War (1861-1865).

Chaucer's nun – The nun appears in Geoffrey Chaucer's (ca. 1343-1400), *Canterbury Tales.*

Algonquins – a group of northern Native Americans

Kirby and Spence – William Kirby (1759-1850), is known as the "father of entomology," which is the study of insects. William Spence (1783-1860), was a founder of the Society of Entomologists of London. Together they wrote *An Introduction to Entomology* (1822).

the Ved – the Vedas, the ancient scriptural texts of Hinduism

Hindoo commentator – The commentator is Raja Rammohun Roy (1772-1833); the quotation is a translation of Hindu scripture.

Thseng-tseu – another name for Confucius

Mencius – Meng Ke (ca. 372-289 B.C.), was a Chinese philosopher, teacher, and follower of Confucius.

"How happy…made them worse." – from John Donne's (1572-1631), poem, *To Sir Edward Herbert*

Conclusion

Yellowstone – a reference to the Yellowstone River, which is now part of Yellowstone National Park

Tierra del Fuego – an archipelago off the southern tip of South America, first sighted by Ferdinand Magellan in 1520; its name means "land of fire."

"Direct your eye…cosmography." – from William Habbington's (1605-1664), *To My Honoured Friend Sir Ed. P. Knight*

the source of the Nile…Northwest Passage – These represent various mysteries in exploration, the answers to which were unknown in Thoreau's time. The sources of the Nile and Niger Rivers were not fully understood until the late 1800s; the source of the Mississippi River, however, was known. The Norwest Passage, the search for a direct route across the Arctic, from the Atlantic Ocean to the Pacific Ocean was not possible then. Thoreau, however, wants his readers to search their own "higher latitudes," which he considers more important and mysterious than exploring the earth.

Franklin – Sir John Franklin (1786-1847), was a British explorer who searched for the Northwest Passage, but disappeared and died trying to find it.

Mr. Grinnell – Henry Grinnell (1799-1874), led an American expedition to find Franklin.

Mungo Park – (1771-1806)a Scottish-born explorer of Africa

Lewis and Clark – Meriwether Lewis (1774-1809), and William Clark (1770-1838), explored the American West. The famous expedition that bears their names took place between 1804 and 1806 and was designed to explore the lands of the Louisiana Purchase.

Frobisher – Martin Frobisher (ca. 1535-1539), was an English seaman who made three voyages to the New World trying to find the Northwest Passage.

South-Sea Exploring Expedition – a U.S. Navy expedition that explored the South Pacific and Antarctic Oceans in the 1840s

"Erret, et…more of the road." Thoreau's translation of Claudius Claudianus' (? - ca. 404), *The Old Man of Verona;* Thoreau changes "Iberians," meaning people from Spain or Portugal, to "Australians."

Zanzibar – an island off the coast of East Africa

"Symmes' Hole" – John Cleves Symmes Jr. (1779-1829), is known for his Hollow Earth theory: "the earth is hollow and habitable within."

Gold Coast and Slave Coast – The Gold Coast is a region in West Africa that is now called Ghana; the Slave Coast is a region that lies to the west of the Gold Coast, so called because it was a major point of departure for African slaves who were brought to the New World.

the Sphinx – According to Greek mythology, the Sphinx was a creature with the body of a lion and the head of a woman; she posed a riddle ("What walks on four feet in the morning, two in the afternoon, and three at night?") to travelers and killed those who gave the wrong answer (The answer is "man."). Oedipus solved the Sphinx's riddle and became King of Thebes.

Mirabeau – Honoré-Gabriel Riqueti, count de Mirabeau (1749-1791), was a French politician and an orator who was influential during the French Revolution.

Kabir – (1440-1518), an Indian mystic and poet

"A living dog…a dead lion" – This quote comes from Ecclesiastes 9:4 and indicates that Thoreau prefers his "modern" society, because it lives, to the mighty or "intellectual" past, because it is dead.

"and lo! creation…view" – from Joseph Blanco White's (1775-1841), *Night and Death*; White was a Spanish theologian and poet.

Croesus – (595-546 B.C.), a king in Asia Minor, considered the richest man in the ancient world; he was defeated by the Persians.

Mameluke bey – a member of the group of leaders established by the Ottoman Empire that ruled throughout Egypt and Syria from approximately 1250 to 1517

Webster – Daniel Webster (See earlier Note, *Webster,* in *Civil Disobedience.*)

Vocabulary

Note that this alphabetical vocabulary list covers all the essays.

abide – to remain or remain strong
abject – lowly; wretched
aboriginal – original; primal
absolve – to clear from blame or obligation
admonition – a scolding or warning
affinity – a liking
alacrity – eagerness; promptness
alburnum – a white, soft layer under wood's visible surface
alluvion – the flow of water
ambrosial – heavenly (According to classical mythology, ambrosia is the food of the gods.)
amelioration – improvement
amity – friendship; peaceful relations
antagonism – hostility
apathies – lapses of caring or concern
apprehend – to understand; to expect
apprehension – the ability to be understood
arduous – difficult; laborious
ascetic – self-denying; shunning food and drink
asinine – ridiculous
askance – sideways, implying disapproval or distrust
assuaged – soothed
atheism – the denial of the existence of God
audacious – bold
auroral – morning-like
austere – somber and grave; strict in discipline
aversion – an avoidance
backgammon – a two-person board game that is played with dice
bantling – *[archaic]* a baby
bard – a poet
bayou – a slow-moving body of water
begirt – *[archaic]* encircled
behooves – becomes; suits
benevolence – goodwill
bereave – to rob
bestowed – given
bivouac – *[archaic]* an all-night military vigil or guard
bough – a branch

bower – a temporary structure covered with leaves and flowers
bulrush – a grass-like plant that grows at the edge of water
buoyancy – the ability to float
burghers – town leaders
capacious – able to receive or contain
capitulate – to surrender
cerulean – sky-blue
chagrins – embarrasses
chanticleer – a rooster
churlish – sullen
clout – a strike, hit, or blow
complacency – contentedness
conciliate – to plead for
confounding – ruining; confusing
congealed – solidified
conjectured – guessed, theorized, or assumed
connives – pretends to be ignorant of; conspires
conspicuous – obvious; prominent
consuetudes – customs
consummation – the ultimate goal
contiguous – bordering
contriving – inventing
conventicle – *[archaic]* a religious meeting that is held secretly or illegally
conviction – a strong belief
convulse – to shake violently
cosmogonal – *[archaic]* relating to the universe
covenants – binding agreements
cumbers – burdens
curricle – a two-wheeled carriage drawn by horses
defiling – soiling; contaminating; corrupting
deify – to worship as a god; to exalt
dejection – sadness
demagogue – a leader who gains power by appealing to people's emotions, especially fear
deprecate – to deplore or belittle
desecrate – to violate or destroy the sacredness of
desponding – despairing
diadems – crowns, jewels
diastole – the relaxation of the heart; opposite of *systole*
dilapidated – run-down; deteriorated
disapprobation – disapproval
disconcerted – confused or shaken

discretion – judgment
disdain – scorn
disencumbering – relieving
dissimulation – deception
ebriosity – *[archaic]* drunkenness
éclat – brilliance or excellence
effigy – an imitation or likeness
eloquent – showing grace in speaking
eminent – outstanding; famous
emphatic – insistent
empyrean – relating to heaven
encroachments – intrusions; trespasses
endeavor – to attempt or struggle
ennuis – feelings of boredom or depression
environs – surrounds
ephemeral – lasting for a brief time; short-lived
epilepsies – seizures or spasms
equilibrium – evenness; balance
eulogies – verbal or written praises for those who have died
evanescent – like a vapor; vanishing
evitable – avoidable
exorbitant – excessive; extreme
exoteric – accessible to the general public
expedient – something that meets a need
expiate – to make amends
extemporaneous – done without preparation; impromptu
ferule – a rod or stalk
festoons – ribbons, garlands
firmament – the sky
flaxen – yellow
fluviatile – living near rivers
foist – to pass off
forsake – to abandon
frankincense – an expensive resin used for perfumes and incense
freshet – a stream of water
frivolous – trivial; silly
garret – an attic
gazetted – announced
genial – friendly; benevolent
girths – straps holding the saddle onto a horse
glaucous – gray
gluttonous – greedy

Godspeed – a parting word used to wish someone good fortune or success
gossamer – very thin, fine fabric
gregariousness – sociability
guile – deception
harbinger – an omen or predictor
heathen – a person who has not been exposed to Christianity
hieroglyphic – symbol or sign
hireling – a person who works only for money
hoary – ancient; gray with age
hobgoblin – a mischievous spirit; a source of problems or harassment
homage – a tribute
homeopathic – taken in small amounts so as to provide immunity
husbandry – agriculture
ichthyologists – people who study fish
imbrute – to make brutal
imparted – gave, transmitted
impertinence – rudeness; showing bad manners
impetuous – hasty; impulsive
impiety – lack of respect
incapacitated – not capable
incessant – not stopping; constant
incredulity – disbelief
indignation – offense; anger
indispensablest – most necessary
indomitable – unconquerable
inducement – an incentive
indulged – allowed; given in to
influx – the process of flowing into
insectivorous – feeding on insects
intangible – unable to be physically touched or understood
integrity – wholeness, unity; authenticity
intercourse – communication between people
intimation – a suggestion
intrinsic – natural; native
invidious – insulting
isthmus – a small strip of land that has water on both sides and connects two larger portions of land
kittly-benders – *[archaic]* the practice of running a sled over thin ice
lampreys – fishes without real jaws that attach themselves to food with a form of sucker
languid – slow; not energetic
latent – dormant; potential

laudation – praise
lucre – money or profit
magnanimity – generosity
manifest – obvious; apparent
martyrs – people who suffer or die for what they believe
maugre – *[archaic]* in spite of
mediocrity – ordinariness
mendicant – begging from others
metamorphosed – transformed
metaphysical – supernatural; not perceivable by the senses
mien – the facial expression
misapprehension – a misconception or misunderstanding
modish – stylish; fashionable
moiling – laboring; slaving
monotonous – repetitive and boring
municipal – relating to local society or government
nettle – a thorn
nimblest – the quickest and most agile
nomenclature – a system of assigning names
nonage – immaturity
oakum – a material made from hemp fibers used to caulk wooden ships
obsequious – overly flattering and subservient; worshipful
obstinately – stubbornly
omnipresent – everywhere; present in all places
ornithology – the study of birds
ostentation – showiness, pretense
palpitation – a trembling
paltry – small amount, meager
paradox – something that contradicts itself
parallax – a change in the perception of an object that results from a new angle of observation
parchment – paper made from sheep or goat skin
parry – to ward off
pecuniary – relating to money
pedigree – heritage
pellicle – a thin film or skin
pellucid – transparent; clear
penances – acts of atonement
permeable – able to be penetrated
perturbation – agitation
petulance – rudeness, insolence
philanthropy – a love of humankind; charitable acts

pipewort – an aquatic herb
piquancy – an attraction; appeal
piques – excites or stirs up
piscine – relating to fish
porticoes – porches
potamogetons – aquatic plants that float on still waters
prate – to babble
prattle – to chatter
predominating – dominating; ruling
profane – low; earthly and trivial
prostitution – cheap, frequent use
prostrate – lying flat with the face down
provender – foodstuff
proximities – relationships to those who are near
prudence – sensible judgment
pules – *[archaic]* whines or whimpers
quadrupeds – four-legged animals
rebuked – criticized; chastised
rectitude – righteousness; morality
redolent – fragrant
reminiscence – a memory
reposes – reclines or relaxes
repugnance – a dislike; disgust
requisitions – requests
residual – what is left behind
reverence – respect, honor
reveries – rhapsodies; pleasant considerations
rhetoric – eloquent speech
rove – to roam or wander
rudiment – the basic part, fundamental
sallies – jokes, quips, or jests
sanction – an approval or allowance
scintillation – a spark
scullion – a low kitchen servant
scurf – the outer crust
sect – a group
sedgy – covered with grass-like marsh plants
selvage – the uncut edge of fabric
semblance – a likeness
sentinels – watchmen, guards
shillings – British coins
shorn – shaved

shriven – absolved
sloth – laziness
somnolence – sleepiness
sovereign – self-governing, supreme; someone who exercises authority
squalid – dirty; wretched; repulsive
stagnant – inactive; not fresh
stipulation – a term or condition
stratum – a layer
sublime – majestic; supreme
substantiate – to make real; give substance to
succinct – brief; concise
superfluous – excessive; having a surplus
superinduces – *[archaic]* brings on in addition
surfeit – an excess
sutler – *[archaic]* someone who sells small goods to soldiers
sward – grass-covered land
sycophantic – flattering; following worshipfully
sylvan – relating to woods or forests
systole – the contraction of the heart; opposite of *diastole*
tafferel – (taffrail) the railing around the stern of a ship
talons – the claws of a predatory bird
tantamount – almost the same as
tempestuous – stormy
tinder – kindling; flammable material
tintinnabulum – *[archaic]* a ringing
titular – existing in title only
transgress – to violate
transient – temporary
trifles – things of little value and/or importance
unconciliatory – hostile, antagonistic
undulating – rising and falling like waves
unfathomed – not comprehended
unrequited – without having the same emotion returned
unscrupulous – unethical; dishonest
unsought – without being looked for
unwieldy – unmanageable; bulky
vagabond – wandering
venerable – worthy of respect and reverence
venison – deer meat or other wild game
viand – a piece of food
victualling – *[archaic]* providing food
virile – relating to a grown man

vitiates – corrupts or debases
vitreous – like glass
volatile – changing quickly
voluptuous – related to pleasure
voracious – ravenous; extremely hungry
wantonly – without restraint
whimsical – fanciful; silly
yore – time past
zephyr – a gentle breeze